FASHION KNITWEAR

FASHION KNITWEAR

Jenny Udale

Laurence King Publishing

LAURENCE KING

Published in 2014 by
Laurence King Publishing Ltd
361–363 City Road, London,
EC1V 1LR, United Kingdom
T +44 (0)20 7841 6900
F + 44 (0)20 7841 6910
enquiries@laurenceking.com
www.laurenceking.com

This book was produced by Laurence King Publishing Ltd, London

A catalogue record for this book is available from the British Library

ISBN: 978-1-78067-343-1

Senior Editor: Jodi Simpson
Copyedited by Virginia Hearn
Picture research by Sarah Hopper
Design by Praline

Printed in China

Frontispiece: Stine Ladefoged, 'Eiffel of Bones' collection
(Photographer: Niklas Hoejlund, Model: Sissel, Styling:
Maria Angelova, Makeup and hair: Gabriella Tipsa)
Front cover: Iris von Arnim, Accessory campaign
(Photographer Anja Boxhammer, Model: Edyta Zajak/MD Management)

Contents

Introduction

This book profiles 40 of the most exciting knitwear designers and companies working in the fashion industry today – menswear and womenswear designers who have developed their love of knitwear into successful high-end brands. In some cases they may have started out manufacturing hosiery, or expanded their product range to also include woven fabrics, but these designers are fundamentally known for their knitwear. Although crochet and macramé are not technically knit, they do use the process of looping a length of yarn to fabricate garments, so designers working with these techniques have also been included in this book. Both new designers and older established companies are profiled; all are designing innovative knitwear in terms of yarn, silhouette, pattern or texture.

Though many fashion brands are designing exciting knitwear within their collections each season – such as Stella McCartney, Issey Miyake, Burberry, Comme des Garçons, Alexander McQueen, Alexander Wang, Vivienne Westwood, Jean Paul Gaultier, Dries Van Noten and Kenzo – they are not known primarily for their knitwear and have therefore not been featured.

To try to get a better understanding of these profiled designers' work, I posed a variety of questions about how their career has developed, what has inspired them along the way and what kind of processes they use within their designs. I also asked them where they see the future of knitwear and their opinions on new technologies used in the creation of knit garments, and how these might be affecting the craft aspect of knit. I have selected images that show all aspects of a knitwear designer's work: knitwear on the body and up close in detail, studio shots and fashion sketches.

While interviewing the designers, it was interesting to discover that many had learned knitting from their parents or grandparents, long before they studied knitwear in higher education. It is encouraging that, in this computer-driven age, craft skills are still being passed on from generation to generation. While the designers look to a variety of fields and media for their research, it is significant that many cited architectural forms as a key inspiration, with the idea that each brick builds upon others to become a three-dimensional structure, as stitches combine to create a garment. Knitwear is one of the few design disciplines in which the designer has complete control of the product they are designing and making, first creating the knitted fabric from yarn and then developing the fabric into the finished knitwear piece.

The uppers of the Nike Flyknit running shoe are machine knitted, a technological innovation that knitwear designers Brooke Roberts and Kylee Davis (see pp. 16, 106) find exciting.

At its most basic, knitting can be a fast way to produce a garment and a portable method that can be used anywhere with only simple equipment.

Changes in trends, technologies and styles have influenced and inspired knitwear designers. The function of knitwear within our wardrobes has changed over the last few decades. Our offices and transport are now climate controlled, keeping them cool in the summer and warm in the winter. The need for light layers in summer and heavy knitwear in winter is less defined. The trend towards less formal dress for work and more time spent working from home makes knitwear a comfortable option, with a knitted piece quite often taking the place of a tailored jacket. No longer required simply for winter warmth, knitwear has evolved into a versatile year-round fashion staple.

In the late 1990s, companies were investing in computer-aided knitwear technology to produce knitted garments more quickly and with a finer finish. These machines could also produce whole garments in three dimensions without any seams, producing both the textile pattern and the shape of the item without any additional sewing or finishing techniques. Issey Miyake used these new processes to develop a garment system called A-POC (A Piece of Cloth). From a continuous tubular length of machine-knit fabric, sections are cut away to reveal various garments. These pieces can then be altered by the wearer, who might cut away further fabric so that a dress becomes a top and skirt, or a long-sleeved top becomes sleeveless. This kind of high-tech knitwear production was innovative, and the idea that the wearer participated in the production process unique. Today many new products are incorporating machine knit technology, such as the knitted uppers of Nike Flyknit running shoes.

Perhaps in reaction to the highly controlled fine machine knits being produced, designers began to use knit in a more artistic, sculptural way. Fashion designers like Alexander McQueen and Jean Paul Gaultier commissioned one-off extravagant showpieces for the catwalk; Sid Bryan from Sibling (see p. 190) made extreme chunky hand knits for Giles Deacon and McQueen. The Swedish designer Sandra Backlund (see p. 184) has also been a major influence on a new generation of designers. Backlund, who cites as an inspiration Yves Saint Laurent's 1965 knitted cocoon wedding dress, is best known for modern, sculptural hand-knit garments, which are photographed in a deliberately futuristic, fashion-centric way to avoid looking 'crafty'. She has inspired many a knitwear student to design something more daring than a new jacquard pattern.

Environmental sustainability is another feature of contemporary knitwear. Fully fashioned knit and seamless machine knitting results in far less waste compared to the production of a woven-fabric garment. A garment cut from cloth and then sewn together results in a great deal of leftover fabric,

This 1965 knitted cocoon wedding dress by Yves Saint Laurent – an inspiration for Sandra Backlund (see p. 184) – is made from white hand-crocheted wool done in several stitches alternating with slotted satin ribbons ending in front bows.

Knit technology is inspiring textile innovation, such as this silicone moulded knitwear by Xiao Li.

while a knitted garment can be made to exact pattern pieces or as a single, complete piece. Also, yarn can be recycled: a garment can be unravelled and re-knit, or the fibre can be recycled and re-spun. Designers like Nikki Gabriel (see p. 160) are working with recycled wool.

New forms of textiles are being developed through knit technology. Smart textiles can change their shape, colour or sound in response to changes in the environment or body such as heat, light, pressure, electricity or heart beat. Knit is good for this as its construction can produce circuits and communication networks through which information can travel. A new type of textile has been created by a recent graduate from the Royal College of Art, London. Xiao Li has created silicone garments that have been moulded from her knitwear – a sort of non-knit knitwear.

Knitwear today is a wonderful mixture of styles and techniques, from beautiful, seamless computer-generated fabrications to extreme sculptural shapes crafted with two needles by hand. The 40 designers showcased here have been selected for their innovative and fashion-led designs. I do hope you enjoy what they are doing and are inspired to look more closely at knitwear in the future – and maybe even to pick up some knitting needles yourself.

Jenny Udale

Allude

Opposite
Textural stitches change
direction in this patchworked
fitted sweater.

Below left
The knit appears to split
and travel around the sides
of this sweater.

Below right
Rich stitch texture has
been created in this
sweater and cardigan.

Andrea Karg has been fascinated by cashmere from the moment she first touched it. Though she studied law at university, Karg left the legal world in 1993 to pursue her love of cashmere and start her own fashion label, Allude, in Munich. Finding cashmere clothing confined mostly to simple V-neck sweaters and plain twinsets, Karg set out to design contemporary, feminine, form-fitting garments. Her first collection comprised 12 cashmere womenswear pieces and has now expanded to over 300 cardigans, sweaters, shirts, dresses, coats and accessories per season. She introduced a menswear line in 2000 and childrenswear in 2004. The Allude label is now sold in more than 30 countries around the world. As well as garments, Allude also produce a line of all-natural products for washing and caring for cashmere – the Allude Care Series.

The Allude collections are classic and sophisticated, with easy, comfortable silhouettes and beautiful design details. Although each piece is timeless, the colour palette and styling keeps the garments fashionable each season. All garments are made from high-quality cashmere. The luxurious yarn is light, warm, breathable and very soft.

Karg uses cashmere in all seasons, both in its pure state and also mixed with other fibres: finely machine-knitted for summer or roughly hand-knitted for winter. She is constantly experimenting with techniques, such as intarsia, and incorporating different materials and fibres into her cashmere designs. Working always with highly skilled craftspeople ensures that Allude collections meet the highest standards of quality.

Above
A lightweight cotton / cashmere mix is used for this soft casual summer catwalk look.

Left
In this sketch of another summer look, a cotton and cashmere bra is visible beneath a fine cashmere sweater.

Why did you start the brand?

I started the brand when I invented the first bodied V-neck sweater in bold colours, some 20 years ago. Cashmere was not known as a fashionable material.

How important is the Allude heritage to the design of each collection?

For Allude I have been creating key pieces with key details. These two attributes have been the main success in the past 20 years. I think this gives our clientele a certain confidence in wearing the products. They know that they are wearing a high-class product with a certain twist of fashion and modernity.

How is the brand developing?

It is expanding. It is now available in 27 countries at 720 carefully selected high-end retailers.

Roughly what size is each collection, and how much of it is knitwear?

The collection has two lines – here the buyers can find timeless basics and also high-fashion pieces. The catwalk collection is made out of several Allude key pieces, like the Allude blazer, and defined with new pieces; some come out of the main collection and some are totally new styles.

What other design disciplines influence and inspire you, and why?

Art for visual and music for emotional creativity.

What is the most inspiring piece of knitwear you have seen?

Each season I am re-inspired by a variety of different knits. I love to experiment with knit – knit is endless; this is my personal passion.

Colour, texture, pattern, silhouette – which comes first?

The process starts with a vision, so the beginning is never defined, which leaves me a wide range of starting points.

Do you have a preference for certain yarns?

Cashmere, cashmere, cashmere!

Craft versus digital – does modern technology help or hinder?

The digital world would not be here today without the old crafts. It is all about the process.

How is the garment silhouette developed?

My inspiration is taken from the female body and the zeitgeist. Season by season I am honoured with a straight view on how I want my collection and my silhouette to look.

Are most of the garments fully fashioned?

This really depends on the look and style I want to achieve.

What machinery produces the knitwear, and where?

We use both Shima Seiki and Stoll machines, plus hand machines in Germany and China.

What steps is Allude taking to address environmental issues?

We look carefully at the ecological balance sheet of each item: for example, we try to avoid shipping yarns around the world for production issues. But as China is the main raw material source in the world concerning cashmere (more than 90 per cent), the product has to travel once from there to the customer.

Creativity comes from…?

…a vision, that through designing you can get onto peoples' skin, which is a huge responsibility and a gift.

Right
An interesting clash of pattern and textures is visible in this ensemble of patchworked skirt, tiger-stripe cardigan and zigzag top and tights. A Lurex yarn used against cashmere gives the gold shine in this autumn/winter cardigan.

Below
Sketch for another autumn/winter look.

Left
The radiating circular zigzag
design in the dress is knitted
using a jacquard technique.
Gold studs have been knitted
into the cashmere scarf.

Below
Detail of the zigzag
jacquard design.

Brooke Roberts

While studying for an applied science degree in medical radiation technology at the University of Sydney, Australia, Brooke Roberts was inspired by the work of some fashion students she met. She previously had had no idea you could do a degree in fashion, and meeting them was a pivotal point in her career. After graduation she worked for a couple of years as a radiographer but was restless. She quit her job and travelled to Europe, enrolling on a couple of short courses at Central Saint Martins College of Arts and Design (CSM) and then on a BA in Womenswear at the London College of Fashion (LCF).

Roberts loved pattern cutting and was naturally good at it because of her ability to interpret two dimensions into three, a skill she had developed as a radiographer. She also had an excellent understanding of anatomy and proportion. She skipped the final year of her degree at LCF and went to CSM to study for a Postgraduate Certificate in Innovative Pattern Cutting.

On graduating, Roberts was introduced to knitwear designer Louise Goldin, and joined her company. She became good at manipulating, cutting and constructing knitwear and worked on the silhouettes, creating the samples with Louise in a knitwear factory in Italy. Three years later, she left to start her own label with a capsule collection of mainly tailored garments with a couple of knitted pieces. The knitted pieces were developed from CT brain scans, and they got an amazing response when she showed them to press and buyers.

The Brooke Roberts collections now consist entirely of knitwear pieces, with 15 – 20 styles each season. Using mostly jacquard and tubular knitting techniques, Roberts develops a wide range of fabrics, from ultra-light and transparent to chunky and heavy, using machines that range from 2.5 gauge to 16 gauge. She prefers making summer knitwear collections because of the delicacy and wider scope in the finer gauges, and her summer collections are as large as, if not larger than, her winter.

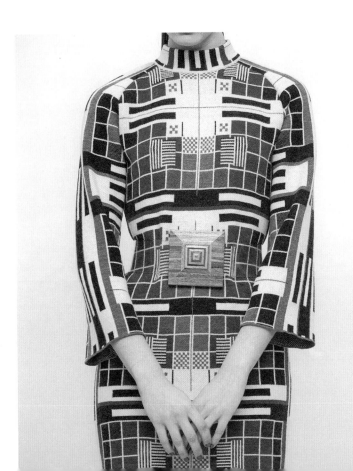

Opposite
The 'Calibration' collection was influenced by the geometry and greyscale in X-ray calibration films.

Left
This outfit was knitted on a Stoll knitting machine with a jacquard program. It is made from cashwool and virgin lambswool. The belts are by EOTWD for Brooke Roberts and are made from reclaimed antique wood and Perspex.

How has your work progressed, season on season?

Every season I employ new knitting techniques and yarns. I am a natural experimenter and do not like to make what I already know works. I like to be surprised by the outcome. Curiosity drives my collections. I explore different medical scans and program them into files compatible with Stoll digital knitting machines. From there I begin experimenting with the yarns and stitches to develop the fabrics. Technological advancements in knitting machines, medical imaging and yarns help my knitwear collections progress each season.

If not fashion, then what?

A DJ. I couldn't live without music.

What other design disciplines influence and inspire you, and why?

I am not so much inspired by design as by science and technology. I have been inspired by the work of architect Zaha Hadid and fashion designers including Thierry Mugler, Pierre Cardin and Paco Rabanne.

Does where you live and work inspire you, and why?

I continue to work as a radiographer, which inspires my work.

How do you choose the yarns you work with? What are your favourites?

I choose yarns depending on the effect I am trying to create. I very rarely use a yarn alone; I mix opposing yarns together, so when I am choosing them I think about how they with react with other yarns.

Craft versus digital – does modern technology help or hinder?

Craft does not exist without technology – it is impossible to create without the help of machines at some point in the supply chain, and we should not be afraid of that. It should not diminish the sense of luxury or preciousness of the product either. I do not subscribe to the idea that something made by hand is inherently more valuable. Cheap labour under duress in the Far East is the first example of how wrong this notion is.

Do you look to the past or the future when designing?

Both, but mostly the future. I recognize that my ideas are a product of what other people have created. It is my interpretation that is new, and depends upon innovation and my use of new technology and materials.

What is the most inspiring piece of knitwear you have seen?

The new Nike Flyknit seamless knitted running shoe (see p. 8). I am also fascinated by the new Adidas Adizero trainers that are knitted on flatbed Stoll machines in a single unseamed upper. Stunningly beautiful and new-tech.

How is knitwear evolving?

Mostly through technology and increased sophistication of programming techniques. Adizero and Flyknit are perfect examples. Knitwear will become less a category of scarves, sweaters and other separates as collections become more directional and high-concept.

Creativity comes from…?

…scientific discovery.

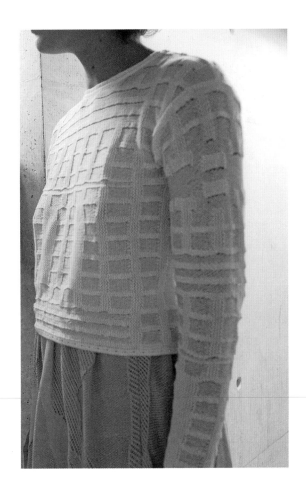

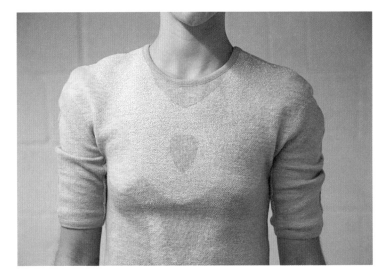

Above left
This white sweater from the 'Wo+Man Machine' collection displays a technique that Roberts developed on a multi-gauge machine. The difference between the yarns in the fabric allows her to create a waffle effect with areas of opacity and transparency.

Above right
For the 'Wo+Man Machine' collection, Roberts looked to 1950s science fiction and imagery from the Allen Institute for Brain Science in the USA for inspiration. The collection was presented during London Fashion Week in a striking performance by fifteen dancers choreographed by Riccardo Buscarini. This blue melange jacquard pique sweater is knitted in extra-fine merino wool and Lurex.

Left
Roberts's studio in Bethnal Green, East London. The bottom right image is of a nissl stain from the Allen Institute for Brain Science, where two Brooke Roberts garments are on display in the foyer.

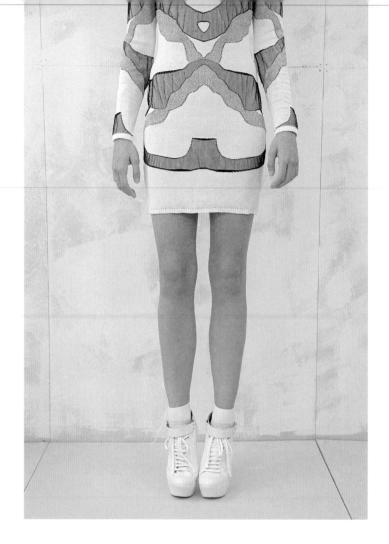

Right and below
The 'Cuts' collection explores the varying opacity and transparency of X-ray imagery. The collection was created in Italy using jacquard and tubular knitting techniques.

Opposite
This dress is made from viscose / elite and monofilament. The pattern is the same as the black and white dress featured, but the doubled layer of transparent yarn on an opaque base has been used in reverse to create a completely different look.

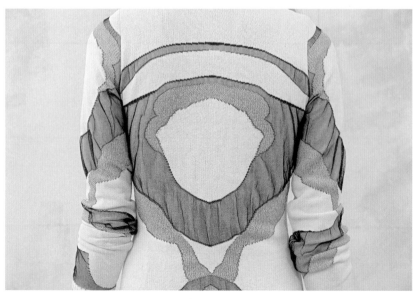

Camilla Bruerberg

Since graduating from the Oslo National Academy of the Arts in 2008, Camilla Bruerberg has worked on various projects for different companies and artists. Based in Norway, she showed her first collection in 2010 as 'debutante of the season' at Oslo Fashion Week. She was then invited to show at Vauxhall Fashion Scout's 'One to Watch: Men' in 2011 during London Fashion Week. She also works at the Oslo National Academy of the Arts, in the knitwear studio.

The Camilla Bruerberg collections vary from 10 to 20 outfits, and she includes woven pieces to support the knitwear to give a full menswear offering. Bruerberg likes to work with flat surfaces during her design process, and so usually starts with the textile. The meeting point between body and textile is her big inspiration, so she often drapes the knitted fabric to find the shape. She finds it interesting to work within the classic men's sweater form, never growing tired of that shape, reinventing it with new yarns and stitch ideas. Most of the garments are fully fashioned and knitted on Shima Seiki machines and Dubied hand flatbeds, along with some hand knit. Bruerberg is interested in producing commercial collections for men to wear every day; however, the practical use is not necessarily always the main focus, but rather her innovative composition of colours, textures and yarns.

Opposite
The 'Archaeopteryx' collection was inspired by traditional Norwegian knit and classic knitwear. This jacquard and intarsia sweater is knitted in a wool with paper core from Sato Seni and a nylon monofilament.

Left
The transparent pattern in this sweater was created with nylon monofilament.

Bruerberg creates the illusion of a garment coming apart but staying in place with areas of opacity and transparency in this intarsia.

What excites you about knitwear?

I love the process of making both the fabric and the garment, and being able to influence the blend of yarns is inspiring. I love being able to control so many factors.

If not fashion, then what?

I think I would have liked to work within natural sciences. I love to learn new things. But then again, I cannot imagine not doing something creative.

Does where you live and work inspire you, and why?

I think where I live is important to my expression. Traditionally Norwegians have a very practical view on things, and this can be both inspiring and provoking. The climate also affects the fashion. For many months of the year it is cold – I guess that affects my choice of materials and shapes.

Colour, texture, pattern, silhouette – which comes first?

Very often it starts with a mood or an idea, reflecting something in society or just a mood I want to materialize. This usually resonates through colours, a yarn or a texture. Finding a new yarn, or rediscovering something old, the making of swatches, combining and diving into the process of exploring a material.

How do you choose the yarns that you work with?

Sometimes I find a yarn that can be a starting point for the whole project, and other times the project dictates what yarns I can use. I visit Pitti Filati to find suppliers, and love to search for new blends and colours. My favourite is a very fine high-twist wool; it is perfect for working with simple but distinct textures.

Craft versus digital – does modern technology help or hinder?

Both. I work a lot with digital tools, but often feel that I should work more with the manual craft to get a deeper understanding of techniques, but if I work with more time consuming manual methods, I feel like it is taking too long and I want to speed it up with technology. I love both; I see only opportunity in the combination of the two.

What is the most inspiring piece of knitwear you have seen?

I cannot choose one specific favourite; it would be a tie between Yohji Yamamoto's big knitwear and Walter Van Beirendonck's fun sweaters (see p. 232).

Do you consider environmental impact when designing and producing your collections?

I think that young designers today cannot easily ignore the ethical challenges in fashion. All my collections are based on wool, which is a renewable resource with good quality and interesting abilities. As a small brand I have freedom and restrictions that are different from bigger companies. I often talk about textile production with customers. My impression is that people really do not know enough about how clothes are made, and I think it is important to help consumers choose good products, both environmentally and ethically.

How is knitwear evolving?

The technology keeps moving forward and the possibilities within knitwear production today really are mind-blowing. I hope it evolves to the point where the potential in the field makes its way to the consumer, and we can think in new ways about production, design and use of materials.

Right
In this sample, Bruerberg experiments with integrating pictures and textiles. A wool / silk rib knit has been digitally printed with an image of an enlarged knit fabric.

Below left
A fine high-twist wool from Sato Seni and a fine silk yarn have been combined to create a mouliné effect and intarsia in this soft oversized sweater.

Below right
This sample has been hand-knitted on chunky needles with leather waste from a previous collection and reused cut-offs from jersey production.

Machine-knitted sweater with a sophisticated mouliné effect and moss stitch.

Camilla Bruerberg   27

Christian Wijnants

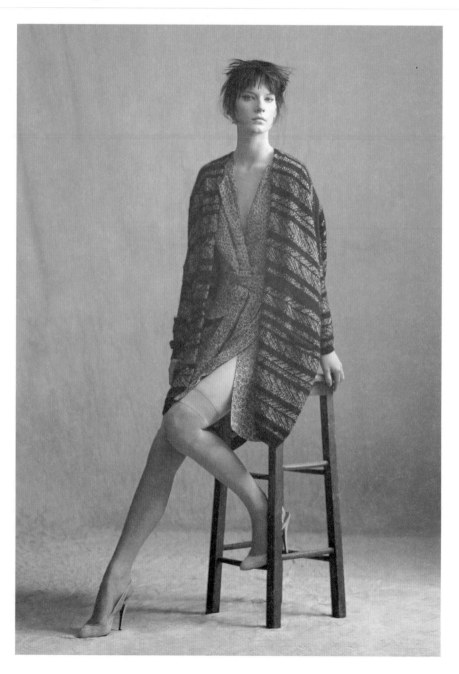

Opposite and above
Oversized easy pieces in a
soft mix of yarns feature in
this autumn / winter collection.
Patterns include knitted
dogtooth and a fine Fair Isle
in a palette of grey, black
and off-white.

Christian Wijnants' career is littered with awards and accolades. He recently celebrated the tenth anniversary of his own label and his collections are now sold in more than 70 stores worldwide.

Originally from Brussels, Wijnants moved to Antwerp to study fashion at the Royal Academy of Fine Arts, where he won the Dries Van Noten Award for his graduation collection in 2000. In 2003 he started his own brand after winning the grand prize at the 2001 Hyères Festival for young designers. In 2005, thanks to the Swiss Textiles Award, Wijnants organized his first show in Paris. In 2006 he received the ANDAM Fashion Award; in 2012 he won the Woolmark European Award and in 2013 the International Woolmark Prize.

Wijnants knitted from a young age, teaching himself on an old knitting machine he discovered in his parents' attic and experimenting with shapes and stitches. He was amazed by all the possibilities of bringing yarn to life, and how he could create his own three-dimensional pieces starting with just a thread.

Wijnants describes his knitwear as organic, natural, feminine and poetic. He is a textile-driven fashion designer and likes to explore other handicraft techniques and mix them with knitwear, such as crochet, hand knitting, macramé, knotting, Tunisian crochet, print and tie-dye.

If not fashion, then what?
Architecture.

Does where you live and work inspire you, and why?
Yes, very much. I like the city. I think Antwerp has a very strong creative scene, and is very inspirational and rich in history. The success of the Antwerp Six inspired a new generation of designers to study fashion. Designers like Dries Van Noten and Ann Demeulemeester inspired me to move to Antwerp and start at the Royal Academy of Fine Arts.

What other design disciplines influence and inspire you, and why?
All kind of disciplines: books, exhibitions, vintage, art, movies, music … basically anything and everything around me can inspire me.

I love Wes Anderson's movies – very poetic, a bit bizarre, full of humour and delicacy. This season I also wanted to pay homage to Aung San Suu Kyi, her devotion, her strength and beauty.

Colour, texture, pattern, silhouette – which comes first?
Usually I work first on textiles for practical reasons. I need to order fabrics and yarns first as they take a while to be delivered. After making a mood board and choosing the colours, I select my fabrics. Only after that do I start draping, moulding and working on designs.

How do you choose the yarns you work with?
I see many different collections of yarns but I often work with the same mills and same yarns. It is nice to create something new from the same base.

What is the most inspiring piece of knitwear you have seen?
Probably an Alaïa dress. Not any one in particular – they are all amazing, the finest knits with great technique.

What knit techniques are important in your work currently?
I recently used a lot of ajouré/lace techniques and printed on top of that. I like to use digital print on top of a special stitch.

Roughly what size is each collection, and how much of it is knitwear?
I make about 50 styles, each of them in different variations, about 150 pieces in the showroom. In the winter half is knitwear, in summer about 30 per cent.

How important is the commercial aspect of your work?
Very. I think it is essential that every piece is wearable and has a certain commercial potential. Of course it is nice from time to time to make special pieces, highlights, but my main objective is that the pieces will be sold and worn by someone.

Also, after making so many collections, I know what people like and do not like, so I am directly or indirectly influenced by that.

Does your work have any environmental impact, and does it worry you?
Yes, the state of our planet worries me. I was raised in a very environmentally conscious way. My mother is from Switzerland, and ecology and respect for nature have been in peoples' minds there for centuries.

In my own way I try to work on qualitative products that are timeless and long-lasting. Also, I think it is our task as designers to educate people to regain respect for handcrafts and clothes in general.

How is knitwear evolving?
It is slow – techniques are often the same, shapes are similar – but I see some exciting things happening. I think there is still so much more to be done.

Creativity comes from…?
…the heart.

Opposite
These two summer looks are knitted with a monochrome abstract pattern.

Left
Sketch from an autumn/winter collection showing ideas for a garment in which the body and sleeves are knitted in one. This type of construction allows Wijnants to experiment with stitches to create curved silhouettes and detailing.

Below
Large stitches travel across the front and curve around the sleeves of this sweater. The sleeve is seamed from the neck down the arm, creating a curved opening.

These two dresses, featuring an innovative tie-dye technique, were part of a collection that won Wijnants the 2013 International Woolmark Prize.

Daniel Palillo

Daniel Palillo was not really interested in education. At college he felt there was too much competition, which led students to make obvious choices in order to succeed and hampered their creativity. He dropped out of college and stopped following fashion. He wanted to create something that was unique and his own, so did not want to be aware of what was happening in the fashion world. He admits that he has not bought a fashion magazine in about seven years.

He says, 'What I do is mostly considered as fashion, but I just do it because I feel that I have to do something and I want to express myself, and it comes out as a form of fashion. I do not consider it as fashion, but others do.'

Palillo's collections consist of mainly unisex jersey pieces with between 150 and 200 styles in each collection. They are bold in silhouette with striking cartoon-style imagery. The designs are made using a cut-and-sew method, where all the pieces of the image are cut and inserted individually into the garment. It is a highly skilled and laborious process. Some styles may have 100 pieces in a single garment. The garments are unlined, so the craftsmanship and complex construction are visible.

What fashion designers have inspired you?
Without Gianni Versace I would not be a designer. When I was 16 years old I loved him. I liked the glamour, but now it is the total opposite: I do not like the glamour at all. I think back then I felt the whole package was really strong – complete Versace.

How has your work progressed, season on season?
I think we are just mastering our things. Hopefully they get better season by season. It is important to tell a continuous story.

If not fashion, then what?
Movies.

Were you a creative child?
I had a wild imagination but I was not creative at all. I grew up with comics, and in the past two years I have gone back to them. The cartoon / comic influence comes naturally to my designing.

Does where you live and work inspire you, and why?
I am based in Helsinki, Finland. Most of the time it is dark here, which I find really inspiring. I feel most inspired in the autumn time when it gets really dark, maybe because in the summer there are millions of things to do, but in the autumn it is too dark to do anything much. If I lived in Hawaii or LA I wouldn't work at all, I would spend all day driving around! I would get nothing done!

How important is innovation to you?
Very important. I want to do things that are new and progressive.

Craft versus digital – does modern technology help or hinder?
I guess it helps. But I am a very craft-minded person.

During my design process there are three steps: first I sketch my ideas by hand, then someone else does a computer drawing based on the sketch and then the factory makes the garment. Things change through the steps, but the changes are always good.

Do you look to the past or the future when designing?
Future.

How do you describe your style?
Random.

Roughly what size is each collection, and how much of it is knitwear?
It is mainly all jersey, 150–200 items. We started doing some knits a year ago, some sweaters and accessories, about 10 styles of knit.

Colour, texture, pattern, silhouette – which comes first?
It depends on the season. Sometimes it is more about creating the shape, and doing some weird forms. We often work with a pyramid / triangular shape to create these forms.

How important is the commercial aspect of your work?
We do not consider the commercial aspect. We tend to put the collection out and if certain pieces become too expensive then it just does not sell or it sells less. It has not really been a problem.

We collaborated with Quicksilver, which was a bit different, but we still had complete freedom in what we did, which was great.

What do you want to do next?
My plan is not to plan. Right now I do what I like to do and I can support myself, so I think the plan is just to have fun.

Creativity comes from…?
…the universe.

Opposite
Garments from the 'Wasted Youth' collection. The dresses, leggings and cardigan are patchworked in cotton jersey fabric. The scarf is knitted in cotton yarns, using an intarsia technique.

Left
The 'Enterprise' collection expresses Palillo's diverse interests – from traditional American sports, to the forests of Finland, to the world of comics – which are manifested in anthropomorphic patterns and slimy imagery. References to the Toxic Avenger and the Marshmallow Man can be found in his imagery. All garments are knitted using an intarsia technique in mohair / wool / acrylic mixes.

Opposite and below
Palillo creates doodle sketches
that inspire his collections.

Right
This sweater and leggings
from the 'Enterprise' collection
are knitted using an intarsia
technique in mohair, wool and
acrylic yarns. The skirt is cotton
jersey fabric.

Eleanor Amoroso

Eleanor Amoroso studied at the University of Westminster in London. She decided to start her own label based on the press she received after showing her collection at Graduate Fashion Week. Since then, she has gone on to show at London Fashion Week and Milan Fashion Week. Amoroso produces incredibly time-consuming large showpieces, but also simpler beautiful handmade macramé-based jewellery. Her first collection was inspired by African and tribal jewellery, and this influence is still apparent in her work.

Opposite
Macramé-fringe dress
with copper pipe detail.

Above
Intricately knotted macramé
dress with dyed ombré fringing.

Although Amoroso's work is often described as 'knitwear', it is actually macramé. Knitting, macramé and crochet tend to be grouped together as they have the same technique in common: they are constructed from a continuous strand of yarn. However, macramé, unlike knitwear, is made up of knots and is knotted entirely by hand. Amoroso admits that, surprisingly, she cannot actually knit and has never studied knitwear. She is inspired by the different textures and silhouettes that can be created with knitwear but is much more interested in surface texture than the technical side of design.

The brand encompasses modern elegance and a tough, darker side – the garments have a timeless quality. The collections so far have been in monochrome, the black or white pieces allowing the eye to focus on the amazingly complex constructions of knots and textures. Amoroso works in an experimental way, weaving unexpected materials into her pieces, such as feathers, chain, beads and copper pipe, contrasting matt and shiny finishes, fluffy and smooth textures.

If not fashion then what?
I've always loved to draw and paint, and almost studied fine art instead of fashion design. It would always be something creative.

Does where you live and work inspire you, and why?
I live in London so I would say it is inspiring to be in such a creative place, yes. It is easy to just pop to an exhibition or look at what other designers are doing.

Where do you find your inspiration for each collection?
I work in an unconventional way, where each piece I make inspires the next. I find the techniques I use very inspiring and as I am working on one collection I often think of new directions I can take it in and already begin to have ideas for future collections.

Colour, texture, pattern, silhouette – which comes first?
For me it is more about the overall feel of a collection. I will develop different techniques initially and as I work be inspired by where they lead. Patterns and silhouette build up from there almost organically. I do not make patterns first; I build the pieces up directly on the stand to see how they work on the body. Pieces often end up quite differently from what I first expected them to be, as I constantly think of new ways to use the technique.

How do you choose the yarns you work with? What are your favourites?
I work with long lengths of fine fringing and vary the volume I use to create heavier or lighter pieces. I find this is the best thing to use, as it is available in long lengths – just a small section of knotting requires a much longer length! The particular fringe I use has a smooth, slightly glossy finish to it, which gives a polished and modern look to the pieces.

What is the most inspiring piece of knitwear you have seen?
I would have to say anything by Sandra Backlund (see p. 184). I am in awe of her work!

What knit techniques are important in your work currently?
I am developing the knotting techniques further to create different textures and effects. The collection I am currently working on is focused on creating monochromatic patterns.

How can macramé – such an old craft – be modern?
For me it is about the way you interpret it. Although I am inspired by ancient macramé pieces, I use modern fabrics and shapes and am always striving to create something new and fresh. I think it is important not to be too literally inspired by it. I use traditional techniques but develop them myself and do things which might not necessarily be considered 'right'. I try to adapt different ways of knotting to bring my own vision to life.

Where do you want to go next? What do you want to do next?
I am keen to move on from creating such dramatic showpieces and adapt my work into pieces that are more accessible, without losing their unique handcrafted charm.

Creativity comes from…?
…inside.

Opposite
This macramé circle top is from an all-white collection of sculptural body pieces. The garment is constructed from multiple hand-knotted hoops.

Above
Unusual sculptural shapes are juxtaposed with floaty floor-length fringing in this spring / summer collection. Twisting, wrapping and spirals around the body form powerful silhouettes, while light fringing creates movement and fluidity.

Right
Sculptural pieces are again apparent in the autumn / winter collection on show here at the 2012 Vauxhall Fashion Scout exhibition in London, but there is a much greater focus on texture, with the pieces being tougher and heavier than her previous work. In contrast, delicate feathers are entwined into the knots to give the effect of fur, and copper hardware details add a modern edge.

This outfit from the S/S 12 show at London Fashion Week is made entirely by hand using long lengths of fine fringing and macramé knotting techniques.

Escorpion

Like many long-standing knitwear companies in Europe, Barcelona-based Escorpion started life as a business that specialized in stocking manufacture. The company José Biosca S.L. was founded in 1929 by a father-and-son partnership. It did not take the Escorpion name until 1954, and it was not until 1967 that Escorpion became known as an exclusive brand for women's knitwear. Escorpion began opening their own stores in 1973 and continued to expand internationally. In 2000 the fourth generation of the family took over the company and totally revamped the business, from the boutiques to their collections, creating a brand that is now known for its elegant, fashionable knitwear. In 2010, the 497° line was born, named after the area of the sky in which the constellation Escorpión (Scorpio, the scorpion) is found. This new line was created to foster creativity and experimentation, in combination with strong design skills and the firm's traditional experience, to create innovative knitwear.

Opposite
This garment from the 'Black Code' collection features asymmetrical ribs and a cross strap detail on the shoulder. It is a mixture of viscose and polyamide yarn.

Right
Taken from the 'Winter Garden' collection, this sweater is a mix of viscose, polyamide, wool and cashmere.

Escorpion designs garments for women, comfortable in fit and luxurious to the touch. Each season the collection features classic pieces of knitwear for everyday, as well as a more experimental line. Escorpion also participates in 080 Barcelona Fashion week. In the recent collections, the design team play with yarns and knit techniques to create innovative textures and silhouettes. The collections have a rich palette, though this may be expressed in strong bold colours one season and subtle metallic tones the next. There is a much purer design vision to 080, and it is these pieces – seen only on the catwalk and not for sale – that showcase Escorpion's directional fashion knitwear.

Left
This dress is a mix of viscose and polyamide yarn with 4% elastane, which gives the garment stretch.

Opposite
A large cable cleverly reduces in size as it travels down the sleeve of this cardigan.

How important is the Escorpion heritage to the design of each collection?

It is very important for us to consider our heritage when we create each collection; without it the collections would lose the character of the brand. It is essential to match the heritage of the brand and design. Our history made our past and will continue to write our future.

How is the brand developing?

We are currently focusing on creating collections in line with the latest fashion trends. We are increasing public awareness of the brand and also expanding into new international markets, such as Germany, Belgium, Denmark, France, Greece, Hong Kong, Israel, Italy, Portugal, the UK, Russia and Lebanon.

You have two other labels as well as the main line. Why do you design these, and what are the differences between them?

Each season we design two lines within the mainline label – a conventional collection and a seasonal catwalk collection. In the past we have also had a few collaborations creating the 497° collection.

Roughly what size is each collection, and how much of it is knitwear?

Two hundred designs, of which 90 per cent is knitwear.

What other design disciplines influence and inspire you, and why?

The design team is always influenced by the latest fashion trends. We are inspired by all forms of art, but the history of our brand is a constant source of interest and influence, shaping the collection each season. At the beginning of each season we travel to main cities like Florence, Paris and Milan to hunt the mood of those vibrant cities. Also, in our office we have a lot of archives from the past that we try to match with the latest trends, and at the same time take advantage of new technology and knitting machines.

Colour, texture, pattern, silhouette – which comes first?

Each one is essential.

Do you have a preference for certain yarns?

In the winter season, we use sophisticated high-quality wool mixed with cashmere and alpaca. In summertime, we use viscose, linen and mercerized cotton in fines gauges.

Craft versus digital – does modern technology help or hinder?

Modern technology is extremely helpful; the most important thing, though, is to let new technology and conventional techniques coexist.

Are most of the garments fully fashioned?

Almost all of them.

What machinery produces the knitwear?

We use the latest machines on the market, like Shima from Japan and Protti from Italy, which help us to optimize our time and costings.

What steps are Escorpion taking to address environmental issues?

In our factory we have a special residual water-treatment system to make sure our dyeing process protects the environment.

Creativity comes from…?

…mixing many influences and daily inspirations.

Left
A dress, in 100% Tactel, from
the 'Colour Therapy' collection.

Below
Knitted using a rice stitch in
a linen and viscose mix, this
dress features an interesting
dart detail at the bust.

Right
In this collection the use of colour therapy was explored, with each outfit on the catwalk a different colour. The show started with this outfit and ended with red, the colour of optimism.

ESK

ESK was launched in 2012 as a fashion and lifestyle knit brand. Creative director Lorraine Acornley (McClymont) completed a BA in Printed and Knitted Textiles at Glasgow School of Art and an MA in Womenswear Knit at the Royal College of Art, London. She went on to design knitwear for companies including Alberta Ferretti, Joseph, Pringle of Scotland, Albam and Connolly. ESK is a collaboration between Acornley and managing director

Stuart Maxwell, who has been running a small family-based knitwear factory for over 20 years. Acornley created ESK to be an aspirational luxury knitwear brand; everything from the yarn and the garment to the branding, the packaging, the web experience and the way shipments arrive has been carefully considered.

ESK has a Nordic feel, whether this comes from Acornley's love of modernism, the furniture she collects, the simple aesthetic or the patterns on the knitwear. The garments are totally wearable and a reinvention of classics, featuring beautiful cabling and Fair Isle patterning in a soft, natural colour palette with sometimes a highlight flash of a stronger colour. ESK garments are made only from natural fibres: cashmere, camel and yak hair, extra-fine merino, silk, Pima cotton and the finest linens.

The collection is currently about 15 pieces of menswear and 20 of womenswear, plus 15 pieces for homewares line ESK Hause. Yarns are sourced from Italy and Scotland, and the collection is produced in ESK's factory in the Esk Valley in southwest Scotland. Though the collection harks back to traditional techniques, the garments are made on the latest Shima Seiki and whole-garment knitwear machines. ESK are creatives backed by a band of artisans and highly skilled local craftspeople with the common purpose of making ESK and ESK Hause the best in their field.

What excites you about knitwear?

I love the whole process. It is like cooking: selecting your 'ingredients', the gauge of machine you want to knit on, your yarn, choosing colours, deciding on the stitch – every one of these decisions is crucial and by changing one you will change the outcome every time. So the possibilities are endless.

Does where you live and work inspire you, and why?

I live in Hertfordshire, just outside of London. I love having the countryside on my doorstep but London only 20 minutes away. Both are equally important to me – the urban landscape and the countryside.

What other design disciplines influence and inspire you, and why?

All aspects of design excite me – architecture, graphic design, fashion, photography. The city, the way we live, the visual landscape, the colours, the lines – all juxtaposed within nature.

What are the differences between designing for men and designing for women?

I have spent most of my career doing both men's and women's knit. I was kind of thrown in at the deep end: Joseph Ettedgui told me I had eight weeks to get my first collection together for him – men's and women's knits. I had studied womenswear so I just got on with it. I love working with the menswear and womenswear collections equally at ESK. Both feed off each other, which is important for continuity. There is always a masculine/feminine edge to my work. ESK men's sweaters look great styled on women.

We have ventured into homewares with ESK Hause and that is really exciting for me, an area I am really passionate about. I guess I design for my own house ultimately. There is a shelter on a summit not far from the factory called Esk Hause. It seemed the perfect name for our homewares line.

What is the most inspiring piece of knitwear you have seen?

While at Joseph I had the privilege of using the vast archive of Miss Deanna in Italy. She manufactured for the likes of Martin Margiela, Kenzo, Joseph and many more. It is the most inspiring archive I have ever seen. I guess I am a visual magpie.

Does your work have any environmental impact, and does it worry you?

We try as much as we can to have as little impact on the environment by using local yarns where possible, as well as reduced packaging, reduced mileage, etc. We are very aware of our responsibilities.

How is knitwear evolving?

I think advances in technology have meant that incredible things are possible, yet we are still wowed by a vintage hand knit. Both have to exist side by side.

There is a definite buzz around UK manufacturing which I am proud to be involved in.

Creativity comes from…?

…observation. From standing still for a moment, breathing in the fresh air and enjoying the here and now.

Opposite
The bottom section and rib trim of the cashmere 'Alexa' sweater is picked out in a highlight colour.

Left
The 'Ewa' sweater is 100%
cashmere, made and milled
in Scotland.

Below
The landscape of southwest
Scotland is an inspiration
to ESK.

Opposite, top
A pattern inspired by Nordic
knitwear works across the body
and down the sleeves of this
sweater, knitted in baby alpaca
in Scotland.

Opposite, bottom
Rough sketches for a
Nordic design, 'Remi'
pants and the 'Simon'
Guernsey-style sweater.

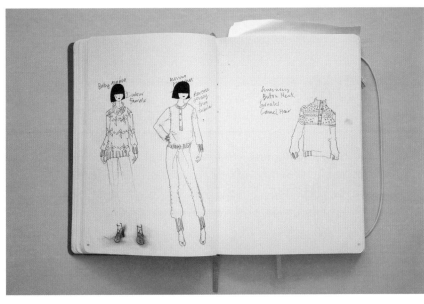

FUTURE CLASSICS©

London-based designer Julie Wilkins started FUTURE CLASSICS© in 2000. The collection featured deconstructed jersey pieces that explored the grammar of the classic T-shirt. Soft tailoring and knitwear were added as the collection expanded each season. The idea behind the label is to continually refine garment ideas that will stand outside of the mainstream, and so create their own classic universe.

When designing the collection, the starting point for Wilkins is always the traditional, fully fashioned knit garment – taking the curves and lines of knitted panel shapes and reconfiguring them into something that feels new while still referencing the original. Wilkins loves multi-wear garments that can be adapted and worn in lots of different ways. She also likes to play with the layering of twin and triplet sets that interact. The knitwear is made in a modern and deconstructed way, often using traditional techniques and fabrics – silk, cotton, cashmere, wool. All the knitwear is fully fashioned, but the interior of the garment is as important as the exterior and often ends up swapping places with it, leaving seams and facings exposed.

Wilkins balances designing collections with writing and recording music, and recently took a sabbatical to complete her second album, *The Electra Woods*, before returning to her label with a newly reconfigured capsule collection based on ten 'must have' items per season.

Opposite
Grass marl twinset fully fashioned in merino wool, with multi-wear adaptable shrug and cape-back flat pack V-neck sweater.

Left
Camel cape-back multi-way cardigan in soft wash wool/cashmere.

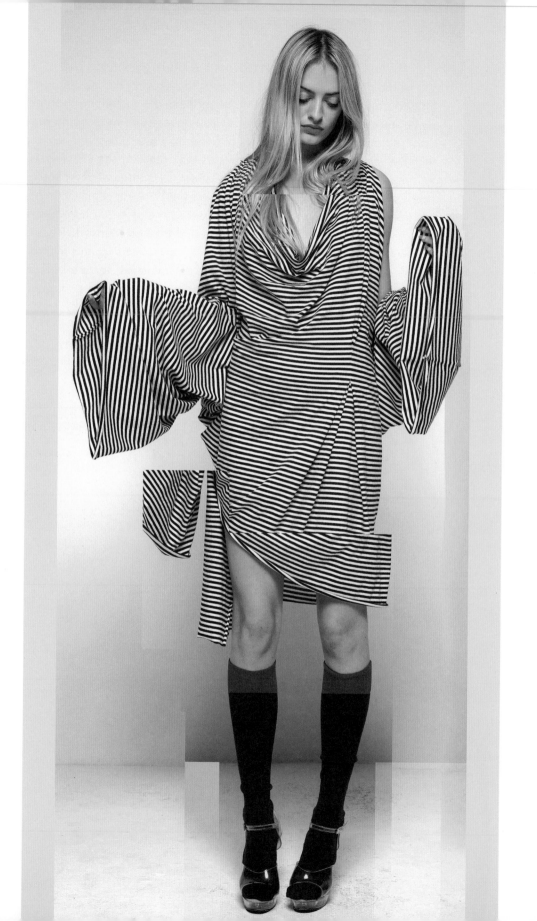

What other design disciplines influence and inspire you, and why?
Sculpture – modern interpretations of what that is. Painting – everything about it. Furniture and carpentry and plates. I love crockery.

Do you look to the past or the future when designing?
Always the past. We are making the future – nothing there yet!

How important is the commercial aspect of your work?
I always start from what I want to wear, and what is functional and wearable but exciting to me. Practically, though, knitwear production is very labour intensive and specialized, and it is really hard to find factories willing to work with you and produce complex pieces with small runs, at a price that is viable.

Does your work have any environmental impact and does it worry you?
I work with natural fibres only, but do produce overseas (UK factories would not take on my work) and so clock up air miles. But we only make to order and use very good factories, and the quantities are relatively tiny.

For me, over-production and the devaluation and misuse of the earth's materials is catastrophic. Textiles outlive humans, so we should only produce well-made, worthy things – not acrylic fashion shells with tiny life spans which will not biodegrade.

Craft versus digital – does modern technology help or hinder?
Technology is the great facilitator – and craft is the manner in which anything is created, the skill to make.

I write electronic music which is totally digital, so I am the craft element in that. I love machines and interacting with them, seeing what comes out of the relationship.

Don't we all talk to our computers now?

What is the most inspiring piece of knitwear you have seen?
My first proper designer knit purchase was about 12 years ago – a Yohji Yamamoto cardigan with cotton fabric front insert panels. It set me thinking about knit construction and started my work in knitting. Disappointingly it did not age at all well, and I later recognized it was cut-and-sew knit, which I do not like. But really, ever since, I have been trying to get across the feeling I had when I met that navy cardigan.

How do you describe your style of knit?
Like everything else I do: radically conservative.

You also design with jersey. Could you explain why this fabric interests you? What kind of jersey do you tend to prefer?
I started with jersey because I could afford to buy 20 T-shirts and cut them up! I loved how you can pull it around and make it do what you want it to, and play with the concept of the classic T-shirt.

I wanted to make jersey expensive and desirable, crafted with as much care as a silk dress, because of what has been done with it – it has become the throwaway fabric to express copyist ideas. I prefer grey marl because it is a neutral modern material. I hate cheap jersey dresses, though.

Creativity comes from…?
…the desire to make what you feel take form – and to display your inner workings in a way that can be shared.

Opposite
Remnant jersey fabric from a previous Breton style was used to create this garment. The cut-out shapes from the old garment formed the seams for the new dress.

Above
This cape-back multi-way
cardigan is traditional in its fully
fashioned finishing and detailing
with fisheye pearl buttons and
Petersham ribbon, but radical
in its construction and the
possibilities of its wear.

Opposite
Grimstone marl catwalk set
consisting of a snood and
oversized twinset. This woollen
body shroud both hides and
reveals the body.

Gaia
Brandt

Gaia Brandt grew up in the countryside in Denmark. Her father built
the wooden house where they lived, with a view of a beautiful lake. The
family did not have a television, and Brandt and her three siblings spent
many hours playing with sticks and stones from the garden. It was a very
open-minded, free-spirited environment, with great possibilities to explore
and be creative.

    Between 1998 and 2001 Brandt trained as a tailor in Copenhagen,
but she then moved to London to study knitwear design at Central Saint

Opposite
These sweaters were knitted on a 12-gauge Dubied machine, then cut and sewn together. The triangular patches were appliquéd by hand.

Below
This grey twinset is an intarsia knit in 100% wool. Brandt finds inspiration in artistic movements such as Dada and Surrealism, exploring the contrasts between illusion and reality.

Martins College of Arts and Design, graduating in 2006. She is now back in Copenhagen running the Gaia Brandt label that she started in 2009. Each collection is still relatively small, but features one-off hand-crafted knitted garments complimented by digitally printed woven pieces.

Brandt's silhouettes are often quite simple, with references to classic men's knitwear. There is also a hint of her tailoring past, with knitted pieces featuring intarsia trompe l'oeil shirt and jacket details including collars, pockets and plackets. The graphic detailing is almost cartoon-like, but the collections remain very wearable as the garment proportions always reference and flatter the female form.

Brandt's collections have a modern feel due to her abstract use of colour blocks and texture within each garment. In one autumn collection, she stitched garments with handmade copper pieces, the metal embellishments adding a hardness and lustre to the soft knitwear.

What other design disciplines influence and inspire you, and why?

Architecture, gardening, vehicle design and photography. I often look at interior design magazines and books to get inspirations for my cloth. I find great inspiration in interiors, where a lot of different styles and objects are mixed together. Colours, plants, wood, steel, light, woollen textures and painted walls gather within the frame of a room.

Colour, texture, pattern, silhouette – which comes first?

I do not know what comes first. I am interested in the composition of materials, qualities, structures, styles and colours, new and old. My work evolves from a base of combinations that cannot be decoded immediately, instead leaving a mysterious and poetic picture of the world we live in.

Does where you live and work inspire you, and why?

Yes, very much. I have my little studio in my top-floor flat in Copenhagen. There is great light and lots of things on the walls and hanging from the ceiling. I have a tendency to collect all sorts of things, mostly vintage. For some people it might be a little chaotic, but it makes me feel at home and safe, with lots of things around me.

How do you choose the yarns you work with? What are your favourites?

I always work with pure materials, lots of merino wool and a cashmere mix. I would like to work with other materials also, like bamboo and some silk combinations, but it can be a challenge with the production. I am still new to the production part of making knitwear.

Do you enjoy the different requirements of designing for spring / summer and autumn / winter?

I am definitely more into the winter season when designing my knitwear. I actually sometimes ask myself if the regular seasons in fashion really fit my process.

Do you look to the past or the future when designing?

I find inspiration in many things from everyday life. Colours, buildings, people, combinations of materials and also the world of art (especially the avant-garde movements, such as Dada and constructivism). Also, nostalgic, old yellowed photographs are a great inspiration. Women with character are a continuous source of inspiration, be they from the past or the present day.

Does your work have any environmental impact, and does it worry you?

I am very worried about the environmental impact of the clothing industry. Working with my collections, I enjoy using second-hand materials mixed with new fabrics, but this is not going to save the world. I think we need effective laws to change these issues in the industry. We will need that in order to have clean water, etc., for the future.

Creativity comes from…?

…a wonderful 'spot' within you somewhere. Sometimes it disappears and it takes a great effort and some new input to find it again. Even looking for it is a creative process, keeping the mind open and ready for whatever this 'spot' likes to be fed with.

Opposite
Gaia Brandt's studio
in Copenhagen.

Right
Collar details were prominent
in this collection. The girl
to the right sports an intarsia
trompe l'oeil collar on her
knitted cashmere top.

A beautifully simple silhouette created in plain and rib knit.

Left
Brandt rarely chooses to work
in monochrome and creates
a wonderful colour palette for
each season's collection.

Below
Collage of inspirational
images: period images that
feel contemporary, Dadaist art,
graphic patterns and lines,
fun details, colours.

Gary
Bigeni

Opposite
The 'Paper Cut Thin' collection
explores the complexities of
emotion through a dynamic mix
of print and texture and a focus
on considered layering. Open-
lattice weave knits reveal what
lies beneath, emphasizing the
depth of layering. This top has
been crocheted in merino wool.

Right
Sweater from the Bigeni Basics
range, knitted in merino wool
and nylon. The stripe detail
travels up the raglan sleeve
to the neck.

Following page
Front and side view of outfit
from the 'Paper Cut Thin'
collection. Bigeni creates
an interesting silhouette with
the tipped curved hem of the
sweater and the draped curved
hem of the dress underneath.

Gary Bigeni has been in love with clothes and colour from a young age, treasuring a two-piece outfit, printed with an array of bright colours, that his mother bought him when he was six. This special outfit was lovingly hung in his mother's wardrobe, out of his brother's reach. Bigeni's colour palette might have become rather more sophisticated over the years, but his passion for clothes and design has only grown stronger.

Based in Australia, Bigeni designs two ranges each season: Gary Bigeni and a diffusion line called Gary Bigeni Basics. The main line sports sophisticated soft tailored and beautifully draped garments that are always designed to be flattering to the female body. Collections are rich in colour and pattern and often combine knit and woven fabrics together in one piece. The Basics range has a younger feel, with simpler shapes and an everyday aesthetic. These garments are mainly made from silk jerseys, tailored leathers and luxurious merino wools. His collections are primarily produced in Australia from natural fibres, and use packaging that is recyclable.

Bigeni's interest in designing flattering silhouettes for women was highlighted when he partnered with shapewear company Spanx at Australian Fashion Week in 2011. During the catwalk show, each model wore a spandex undergarment that enhanced their figure in particular ways, based on the specific Bigeni outfit they were wearing. The Spanx product details were then listed in the show programme, making it easy for women to put the two products together for the most flattering effect.

What has been your career path so far?
Immediately following my graduation from the East Sydney Design Tech in 2002, my designs attracted the mentorship of Australian retailer and fashion icon Belinda Seper. With Belinda on side, my label gained momentum over the seasons and has continued to garner adoration from stockists across Australia and internationally.

If not fashion, then what?
If I didn't work in the fashion industry I would want to work with children, ensuring our next generations are driven and proud to be individuals.

What excites you about knitwear?
The craftsmanship and how you can execute a range of styles fascinates me.

Does where you live and work inspire you, and why?
For me it is more about the surroundings and atmosphere that you create – my studio is filled to the brim with imagery and books of varying creative genres.

What other design disciplines influence and inspire you, and why?
Besides knitwear I focus on draping and tailoring disciplines in my collections, as this mix of soft, fluid, artful lines and multi-dimensional tailoring offers endless inspiration.

Colour, texture, pattern, silhouette – which comes first?
Definitely silhouette – for me, form is where it all begins. I drape directly onto a mannequin and base all designs from this process.

How do you choose the yarns you work with?
I choose based on the techniques of the design and the best way to execute the design through the fabrication.

What are the differences in designing for your two lines?
Bigeni Basics is about clean and simple cuts in my knitwear, whereas with the main line I play with fabrics that can mix with knitwear (e.g., silk and leather), colour and print. All knit garments from Gary Bigeni and Bigeni Basics are fully fashioned.

Craft versus digital – does modern technology help or hinder?
Craft. I have always been very hands-on with my design process. I use modern technology for research purposes, but imagery is always printed, cut out and mounted to mood boards – which is very practical.

What is the most inspiring piece of knitwear you have seen?
Shaping in knitwear always inspires me – seeing beautifully draped knitwear which utilizes the new technologies available.

Roughly what size is each collection, and how much of it is knitwear?
My collections are approximately 45–50 pieces, about 10 per cent being knitwear focused. With a key market in such a warm climate, I need to always be aware of the Australian customer.

How important is the commercial aspect of your work?
It is very important to have a product out there and across many demographics. I ultimately want to be always crafting wearable and exciting clothing for women.

Do you consider environmental impact when designing and producing your collections?
Yes. I work with a lot of natural fibres in both collections.

How is knitwear evolving?
With new technologies for design and production, I think there are now endless ways to incorporate them into a collection – whether it be for spring / summer or autumn / winter.

Creativity comes from…?
…whatever you see around you.

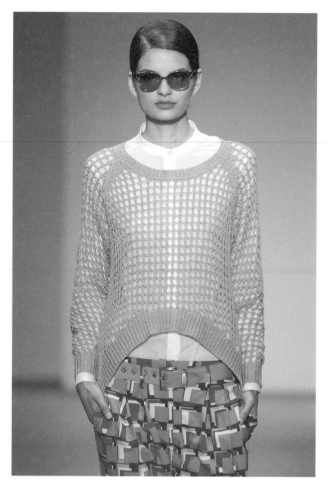

Left
Cotton and rayon mix
lightweight sweater from
the 'Fractured Appearance'
collection. The zigzag pattern
in the knit works with the
graphic-print trousers.

Above
The 'Fractured Appearance'
collection moves away from
Bigeni's signature draping
towards cleaner lines. This top
is hand-crocheted in a linen and
rayon mix for summer.

This outfit combines knit, leather and jersey in a vibrant, earthy colour palette. The stripe in the sweater is cleverly engineered across the body and sleeves.

Iris von
Arnim

Opposite
This boxy hand-knitted sweater, knitted in cashmere ribbon yarn, features a palm tree intarsia.

Below
A batwing top with a bright asymmetric colour-block detail.

'Reduced knitwear design' is how Iris von Arnim describes her collections. For more than 30 years she has been designing and producing cashmere knitwear from her design studio in Hamburg, Germany. Iris von Arnim remains an independent company – the entrepreneurial freedom and lasting quality this brings mean more than growth at any price. The brand stands for tradition, craftsmanship and uncompromising quality. Iris von Arnim stores are located in Munich and the island of Sylt, in northern Germany, as well as in Berlin. In addition, the collection sells to over 200 independent boutiques and department stores worldwide.

The Iris von Arnim collections combine tradition and craftsmanship with modern technology in wonderfully soft yarns. Details such as ribs and cables are very much part of the signature style. Each collection includes about 80 – 100 pieces and consists primarily of knitwear, but also includes woven cashmere double-face coats and skirts, silk blouses and a few trousers. It is not designed to follow seasonal trends but features timeless, classic yet innovative pieces, with each collection building upon the last, creating a flow of design. Von Arnim researches what has worked and what has been well received by customers and takes these pieces and develops them further. The design team wear the samples they have designed as soon as they come in, to see if they feel right and look right. She finds this is the best way to test the desirability of each collection. Designing knitwear that women want to wear is of the utmost importance.

How has your work progressed, season on season?

Good design requires life experience, or, as we say in German, a life lived. The more you have experienced and seen, the better you understand what we really need or feel well in. For me, it was learning by doing. I had no training in design, nor was I surrounded by luxury clothing during my childhood. In my early thirties, I owned a pair of jeans and some scratchy sweaters. There was room for my taste to develop and grow. In the late 1970s I started off with, and became famous for, multicoloured intarsia sweaters, but I got tired of them. I had the urge to design plain sweaters. From that time on, I started with cashmere, but it was always still about what would I like, and what am I missing in my wardrobe?

How do you choose the yarns you work with? What are your favourites?

When it comes to the material, I first need to touch it. The quality and feel always matter first. It is the basis of every piece. We only use the best yarns from Italy and Mongolia. We know where our yarns come from, and we travel often to Italy or even China to review where and how they are produced. We always have cashmere in all kind of shapes, colours and plies, as well as yarn blends such as merino/silk, merino/cashmere or merino/alpaca.

What excites you about knitwear?

You create the surface, the look and the style. You don't just buy a fabric and drape it, but rather develop everything yourself from the surface to the actual piece. Plus, it just feels good on your naked skin.

Colour, texture, pattern, silhouette – which comes first?

We take a classic shape as the basis, upon which the designs are built. That is the start of the process. Never lose sight of who you are designing for.

How important is innovation to you?

I like to work with young designers, both male and female, because the exchange between the gender and generations is important to me. It should inspire but not dominate. Change is important to me when it means development and improvement and fits the brand identity; change for the sake of change is the wrong track. My team and I are always searching for ways to perfect something further. It is a never-ending endeavour.

Craft versus digital – does modern technology help or hinder?

Craftsmanship and modern technologies are not mutually exclusive but complement each other quite well. Nowadays we can implement designs with modern technology, whether with circular-knitting or 16-gauge intarsia machines, which we were not able to do before with our hands or hand-knitting machines. Nevertheless, handcraft plays a substantial role in knitting – whether it is the simple feel and look of multi-ply ribbon yarns, huge stitches or crochet work and embroidery – it stands for luxury and authentic characteristics. We produce in China sometimes because they still have hand machines that no longer exist in Italy. These machines create a different feel from the standard automatic machines.

Creativity comes from…?

… inspiration and fantasy, with a touch of real life.

Opposite
Cable knit scarves have been layered on top of a cape to create a strong silhouette in this styled shoot.

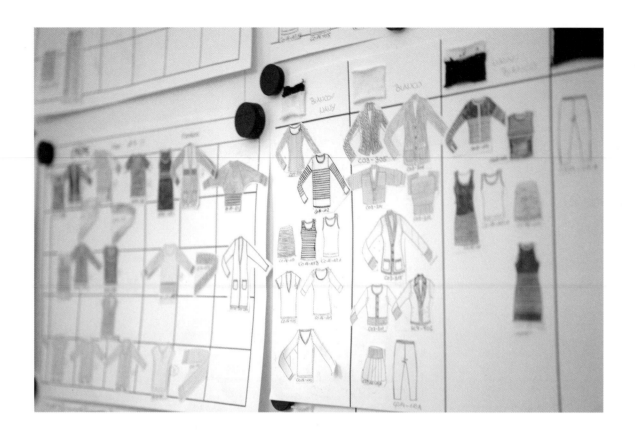

Above
Sketches for a range plan.

Right
Detail of cable and flat stitch
knit structure with a hand-
carved horn button.

Opposite, left
This shawl-collar coat features
a beautiful mix of stitches.
The front panels have been
knitted sideways, creating a
herringbone effect. The pockets
have been highlighted by
a change of stitch, which
is echoed on the sleeve.

Opposite, right
The large cable details travel
down into the peplum of this
hand-knitted cashmere top,
which is worn here with a
reversible, double-faced, two-
colour cashmere circle skirt.

James Long

Opposite and below
The sweaters designed for
the Topman collaboration
were inspired by James Long's
previous work. They were all
machine-knitted in Great Britain
using British yarns.

Following page
'Divine' hand-knitted sweater.

James Long graduated from the Royal College of Art, London, with an MA in Menswear specializing in accessories design, and launched his first menswear and accessories collection at London Fashion Week in 2007. He won the very first NEWGEN MEN sponsorship initiative in 2009, and in 2012 the first Fashion Forward Menswear award from the British Fashion Council. Along with innovative knitwear, the James Long collection includes great outerwear, denim, embellished T-shirts and bags. For the last three years Long has acted as design consultant for high-end luxury brands; he has also worked on limited-edition pieces and collections for Colette in Paris.

Gordon Richardson and Topman have been very supportive throughout Long's career. Long has designed an exclusive collection of leather bags for Topman and recently designed a capsule collection of knitwear. The Topman collection was a great opportunity to bring the best elements of previous James Long collections into one capsule British-made collection.

Known mainly as a menswear designer, Long also designs womenswear and successfully launched his first full womenswear collection on the catwalk in autumn / winter 2011. His womenswear is as eclectic and innovative as the menswear line and contains crossover pieces with a female fit. Long has a painterly approach to his knitwear, combining splashes and strokes of texture and colour that create wonderfully tactile garments.

How would you describe your knitwear?
The more yarns, the more colours, the more techniques, the better. It comes from a non-technical approach; I design it before knowing how to make it. I think it makes it free and new. There are very few constraints.

As well as your own brand you work on consultancies?
I really enjoy working on consultancies; it gives me the opportunity of working in a different way and seeing the process in which other companies operate. I work on full collections, not only knitwear.

If not fashion, then what?
It was always going to be fashion, really.

What excites you about knitwear?
I like the fact that you can create amazing colour and it is so personal. I also like the technical side of it, and the mistakes are important.

Does where you live and work inspire you, and why?
Yes, I live and work in Hackney, London. I think I would be a very different designer if I worked elsewhere. You absorb what is going on around you.

What other design disciplines influence and inspire you, and why?
Music because of the mood, art the creation – all of them, really. Sometimes there isn't a reason why, it just does!

Colour, texture, pattern, silhouette – which comes first?
It is best when they all come together, but it does depend on what I am designing. I do not really have a code or any rules.

How do you choose the yarns you work with?
Once we have established what the collection is about, my team and I will try lots of different combinations and come up with something that we think is modern and new.

What are the differences in designing for men and women?
Mainly the different body shapes; the process is the same, really. It is about awareness of bodies.

Craft versus digital – does modern technology help or hinder?
It helps but you need to have a respect for the craft in any discipline.

What is the most inspiring piece of knitwear you have seen?
The first jumper my mum knitted for me; it inspired me to use knit in my collections.

Roughly what size is each collection, and how much of it is knitwear?
There are 10 pieces of knit in a 40-piece collection, but each season is different for me. It depends on the mood, the feel and what we are working towards on that particular season. Winter has more knits.

How do you develop your garment silhouette?
Lots of design development and fittings on real people.

What machinery produces the knitwear?
It depends what is available, what season it is and what the look of the season is.

How important is the commercial aspect of your work?
Very – fashion is ultimately to sell clothes that are desirable. I do not want to design something that no one wants to wear.

Do you consider environmental impact when designing and producing your collections?
Yes, but fashion is difficult as it is a luxury not a necessity.

How is knitwear evolving?
I think the fabric and expectations of the nature of knitwear are ever changing. The boundaries of what can be achieved with knit are being pushed out.

Creativity comes from…?
…a brilliant team.

Above
Sketchbook page showing details from a spring/summer collection inspired by Edward James's Surrealist sculpture garden Las Pozas and Brian Eno. The swatch is a hand knit and combines crochet and knit.

Right
Machine-knitted sample that has been printed with a devoré technique, creating alternating areas of semi-transparent and opaque knit.

Far right
Machine-knitted sample from a men's autumn/winter collection. The knit is used in reverse, showing the back of the stitches.

This autumn/winter menswear collection was inspired by John Waters and the art of marquetry.

Johan Ku

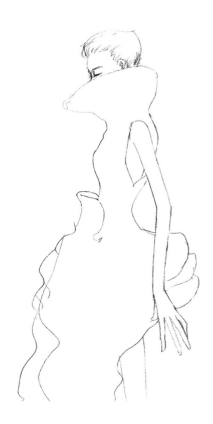

Opposite and above
The 'Re-sculpture' and 'Emotional Sculpture' collections were inspired by the soft sculptures of Claes Oldenburg. Ku describes these garments as 'wearable art'. This textural dress from 'Re-sculpture' (opposite) was created using a hand-operated knitting machine combined with hand crochet and needle punch, using multiple materials. From 'Emotional Sculpture', this dress (above) is hand-knitted in merino wool. Large cables and tucks create a dramatic silhouette.

Above right
A sketch for the 'Emotional Sculpture' collection.

Johan Ku was born in Taipei in 1979. He majored in advertising design at school and started out as a freelance graphic designer. An interest in the fashion and textile industry led him to leave China and complete an MA in Fashion at Central Saint Martins, London, in 2009. While studying, his 'Emotional Sculpture' collection won Gen Art's Design Vision Avant Garde award in New York. After a brief time freelancing, Ku started his own label in 2011. The Johan Ku label is known for its sculptural silhouettes using extremely chunky yarn and chunky knitting techniques. Ku produces two main collections each season: his Gold label, which he describes as his wearable art line, and the ready-to-wear Gray label, which is more commercial. There is also the Purple label for knitted accessories.

Through his knowledge of the textile industry in Taiwan, Ku has been experimenting with artificial fibres and cloth and has developed a new light-sensitive glow-in-the-dark yarn. Under normal lighting conditions, the yarn behaves like a standard yarn, giving the knitted garments their silhouettes, draping qualities and texture. However, in the dark the garments are transformed. By mixing glow-in-the-dark yarns with plain yarns, Ku cleverly shows the garment's stitch pattern and different layers with amazing effect as they glow a futuristic green or violet. Digitally printed fabrics have featured each season in his collections, either as oversized trompe l'oeil knit stitches or as a digitally manipulated abstract knit pattern.

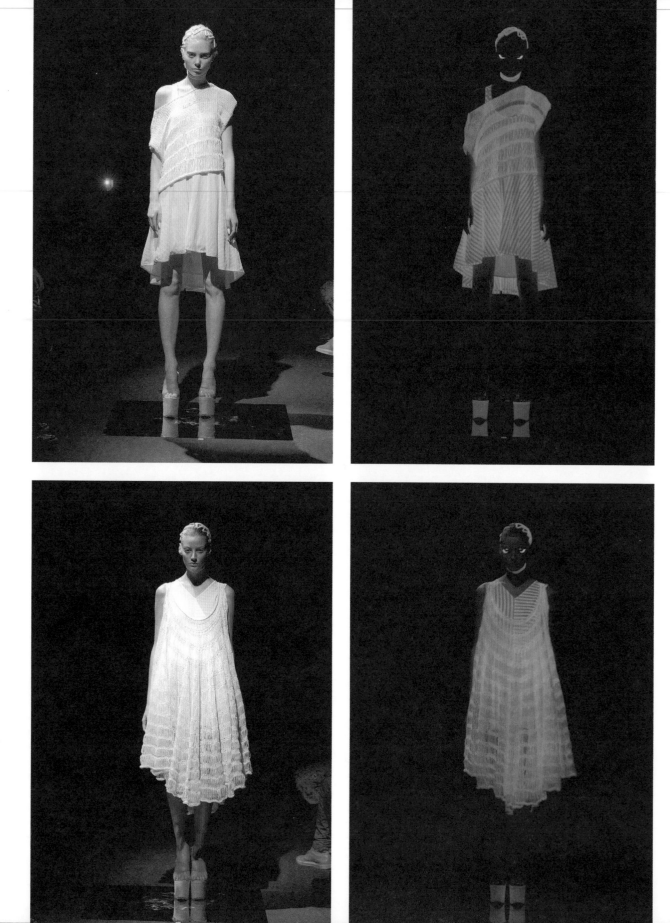

What excites you about knitwear?
It is a hybrid of both textiles and fashion, but also crosses boundaries with other art forms, as exemplified by my 'Emotional Sculpture'.

If not fashion, then what?
I have always liked working with textiles, but graphic design, drawing and artistry has always been my second love.

What influences and inspires you, and why?
I actually studied advertising design before I learned textile and fashion. All my foundations and knowledge in design were built during that period. It's hard to say exactly how it affects my style now, but it definitely influences me imperceptibly. I am hard-working like a typical Taiwanese person, but culturally and ethnically I think I am influenced by the Hak-kâ blood of my mother.

Does where you live and work inspire you, and why?
Not really. A good movie or a special yarn might inspire me more than where I live and work.

What is the most inspiring piece of knitwear you have seen?
The first jumper I had from my mother. It was chunky and warm and lasted for years. I think it was white.

Roughly what size is each collection, and how much of it is knitwear?
It is around 60 pieces every season. Roughly 60 per cent of the total items are knitwear in autumn/winter, and 40 per cent in spring/summer. The others are cut-and-sewn items and accessories.

Colour, texture, pattern, silhouette – which comes first?
Colour is always the first thing to be decided in my collection. I then draw some rough sketches and knit the shapes. I drape the piece I knit on mannequins to do a further adjustment and try to find a new silhouette.

How do you choose the yarns you work with? What are your favourites?
I choose the yarn that inspires me. The glow-in-the-dark yarn is my favourite recently.

How important is innovation to you?
New innovations are very important for me, as I am always looking for new materials or techniques to put in my collection.

Do you enjoy the different requirements of designing for spring/summer and autumn/winter?
I enjoy doing an autumn/winter collection more than a spring/summer one, to be honest.

What are you working on at the moment, and what do you want to do next?
I am working on a spring/summer collection, along with collaborations with the National Theatres of Taipei and Paris. I want to keep my career going and developing my brand here and abroad. I just need more sleep and good health to help me achieve my objectives.

How can knitwear be modern?
It becomes modern when someone modern wears it.

How is knitwear evolving?
It keeps developing with new materials, yarns and technology.

Creativity comes from...?
... experiences and experiments.

Opposite
'The Two Faces' collection was inspired by the film *Enter the Void*. The yarn used in this collection glows in fluorescent light, revealing hidden knit patterns and transparencies. Garments that look tonal and textural in normal light become futuristic with graphic patterning and neon colouring in fluorescent light.

'The Hole' collection was inspired by an art-house film by the same name. This large hand-knitted piece can be worn in multiple ways.

Julia Ramsey

Julia Ramsey's career path so far has been a mixture of designing knitwear for the corporate fashion world and hand-crafting her own personal collections. Currently she is in the process of developing hand-knitting patterns for her 'Pelt' collection, as well as a line of accessories. She is also working on another installation-based knit exhibit, or 'dress-scape', as she calls them. Ramsey's style of knit is sculptural, yet sensual, in both surface texture and silhouette.

Ramsey tries to communicate her personal passion for the potential inherent in all raw materials. Having recently learned to spin the yarns that she knits with, she feels more fully in tune with the entire creative process. She uses undyed organic wool in combination with naturally coloured alpaca, sourcing fibre through local farms, as well as from small fibre producers in Bolivia, to create lusciously soft singles yarn with a neutral, painterly colour effect. She also loves to experiment with materials not necessarily used for knitting, like seam binding, spooled laces or plastic threads, giving her endless textures, colours, sheens and elasticities to play with.

Ramsey splits her time between her hometown on the Eastern Shore of Maryland and Brooklyn, New York. In Maryland she explores the local plants and marsh grasses, observes the paths of snow geese and bald eagles, and rises with the sun to long days of quiet handwork. Back in Brooklyn, the city inspires her with its abundant opportunities for community collaboration, visual stimulation and intellectual engagement.

Craft versus digital – does modern technology help or hinder?

Electronic knitting machinery and its software are remarkable tools for developing innovative knit structure, especially when creating fine-knit garments that are virtually impossible to hand knit. I am fascinated by these machines and would love the chance to use them more. I was lucky to have been trained to program several Shima machines during college, an experience that helped me gain a far deeper understanding of technical knit structure.

Modern technology, though, can be a double-edged sword. I have to be careful not to get sucked into the distractions of the computer world, especially under the guise of its being 'faster'. In the end, if you give proper attention to your task, handwork can be just as quick.

How do you develop your garment silhouette?

My garment's silhouette evolves in response to how the fabric drapes on the body. The whole process is a silent conversation between the raw material, the knitted structure, the human form and myself. I never try to pre-determine a design through sketching. It is much more exciting to discover a solution that could never be imagined on paper.

What are your favourite yarns?

Right now I am spinning my own yarns; they are so beautiful to touch and to knit with. For more standard yarns, Aurora Silk based in Oregon has beautiful peace silk varieties imported from India; Jaggerspun in Maine has a line of organic super-soft merino; and the yarn store Habu in New York City has a wonderful selection of inventive Japanese creations. I try to stay local and natural or source from companies who are invested in handcraft and the environment.

How important is the commercial aspect of your work?

Commerce has very little personal importance to me. I do my best work when I am able to follow instinct and leave fashion trends far behind.

Does your work have any environmental impact, and does it worry you?

The negative environmental impacts of the fashion and textile industries create a significant cause for action. When I contributed to companies who worked with little regard for the earth, it created huge discord within me. I have since made a commitment to work only in collaboration with companies who are dedicated to furthering social and environmental change within the industry. I passionately believe that change is necessary, and I am a much happier person by giving my full (not just partial) support.

Within my personal work, I try to minimize my impact as much as possible. While this can be an extremely nuanced task, I use my best judgement, and I choose to care. I work with dead-stock materials, organic fibres, natural fibres and natural and/or low-impact dyes. I produce my products by hand with utmost respect for the craftsmanship of others and myself. I consider it a lifelong learning process that I am committed to. Greater knowledge about where our products come from and how they are produced leads to a deeper, reverent appreciation for our natural world and for the products themselves.

Creativity...?

...exists. We simply tap into it.

Opposite
Each piece in the 'Pelt'
collection is a 'second skin':
a source of comfort, a temporary
shelter, a reminder of an
animal's gift.

Left
'Engaged' is an installation exploring a modern woman's ambiguity towards marriage through two different wedding gowns: 'In the Air', a knitted dress which was displayed suspended above the ground, and 'Tied-Up' (shown here), a crocheted gown bound in a web of ribbon and silk – two outlooks on the trappings of an age-old tradition.

Below
Detail of 'Tied-Up', in hand-crocheted ribbon and peace silk.

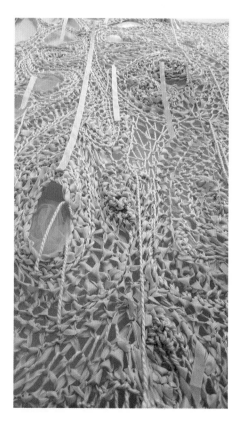

Above
Ramsey's design studio,
Philadelphia, USA.

Left
Hand-spun, organic merino wool
and naturally coloured alpaca
are some of the yarns favoured
by Ramsey.

Julien
Macdonald

Julien Macdonald's career in fashion started with a BA in Fashion and
Textiles at the University of Brighton, UK, and an MA in Knitwear at the Royal
College of Art in London. He was a knitwear designer with Karl Lagerfeld
at Chanel and then head designer at Givenchy. His own label has been his
main focus since leaving Givenchy.

Macdonald always begins the design process each season with a fresh
new inspiration and woman in mind; as trends in fashion develop, so does
his work. He says he tries to develop his style of knit for each season but one
thing always remains the same: glamour. It is fundamental for Macdonald
to make the woman wearing the garment feel sexy and fabulous. Working
with a mixture of old and new lace techniques and super-stretch yarns, he
produces knitwear with an open-knit stitch effect that fits beautifully to the
figure. All of his knit is made in-house at his London atelier and is created
on all different kinds of knit machinery, depending on the techniques being
used in each garment.

Over the past few years, Macdonald's company has developed into
an exclusive bespoke brand. He produces seasonal collections but also
works with private clients and celebrities one on one to give them a unique
experience.

102   Julien Macdonald

If not fashion, then what?

It is hard to imagine a career out of the fashion industry after this long, but I have always had a passion for music and so I would probably be in the music industry.

What inspires you, and where do you find your research?

It is hard to define what inspires me, as my inspiration could come from anything – from an exhibition I have visited at the Royal Academy of Art to the colours in a market stall in Marrakech! Art galleries are always a key source for my research and London has some of the best exhibitions in the world. I also like to keep track of new interior and art books, as they are full of innovation and creative ideas.

Does where you work and live inspire you, and why?

Absolutely, living in Notting Hill in London is great for inspiration. Portobello Road market is thriving with antiques and vintage pieces that spark creativity. I like to spend research days strolling the market and purchasing new and old items to inspire my collections.

Colour, texture, pattern, silhouette – which comes first?

All of these factors are key to creating an interesting and modern collection, but as I started my career studying textiles, I am always drawn to pattern and print as a starting point. I have a passion for decorative arts and textures. Surface design and knit are what my collections revolve around, and the silhouettes and colours develop from that.

How do you develop your garment silhouettes?

We start with creating knit swatches that are influenced by my research, and then we wrap them around a mini-mannequin. From this we get an insight into how the garment will look as a full piece. I am able to then look at the lines of the body and design the full silhouette from this point.

How do you choose the yarns you work with? Do you have any favourites?

When choosing yarns, I call in yarn cards from all the yarn suppliers that we work with in a variety of stretch and stretch blends. Stretch yarns have a high presence in my collections as they help to achieve a bodycon effect that keeps the knits slimming and sexy. My favourite this season is a velvet stretch yarn in bright colours and a metallic coated viscose.

Roughly what size is each collection, and how much of it is knitwear?

I tend to aim for a 30–40 piece collection, and knitwear covers roughly a third of this. It remains a key element of each season for me and works in well with the evening gowns.

Craft versus digital – does modern technology help or hinder?

The craft of knitwear still has a big relevance in modern-day fashion knit design, and I try to collaborate this with modern knitwear technologies. Season by season I research what is going on in the knit world and find inspiration through this.

Creativity comes from…?

…within. It is the air that you breathe, the vision that you see. It can come from everywhere; you can see it on the street and within the people that you meet throughout life's journey.

Opposite
The 'Broadway' dress, inspired by research into armour, was made using a knitted plaiting technique with metallic Lurex and velvet yarns. It was knitted first, then hand-embroidered on top of the knit.

This body-conscious dress is made from a stretch viscose and cotton blend yarn. Inspiration for this piece came from tropical islands and the colours of the flowers that can be found there.

Above left
This 'Renaissance' dress from
the 'Viva Las Vegas' collection
is inspired by 1940s Vegas show
dresses. It is knitted from Lycra
and velvet yarn with Lurex and
chain embellishment.

Above right
The 'Vdara' jumpsuit is knitted
in velvet yarn with viscose on
the reverse.

Kylee
Davis

Kylee Davis's knitwear is a little bit conservative and a little bit quirky. Whether she is using the 'wrong side' of the fabric as the right side or knitting evening gowns, she creates her designs through a juxtaposition of styles.

Davis studied fashion at the Institute of Fashion Technology in Auckland, New Zealand. During this two-year certificate she won New Zealand's most prestigious fashion award – twice – which enabled her to start her first business partnership and label, Insidious Fix, at the age of 20, specializing in New Zealand–made knitwear through her own manufacturing plant. Insidious Fix developed a cult following across New Zealand and quickly became one of its most recognized knitwear labels. The partnership split, however, and she was backed to start a new brand, Stitch Ministry. Although knitwear was a core part of this brand, it diversified into wovens and was also predominantly produced off-shore.

In 2011, dissatisfied with the direction Stitch Ministry was taking, Davis launched a ready-to-wear label under her own name, exclusively producing knitwear. Her first collection was picked up by Browns in London. She produces two collections each season, one for the northern and one for the southern hemisphere. For the production of her collections she works closely with home knitters using needles or domestic machines, which helps incorporate a number of artisan techniques, but she also works with commercial factories who have the latest technology including flatbed, circular and whole-garment machines and digital printing.

Does where you live and work inspire you, and why?

I currently work primarily from home, which enables me to spend more time with my two young children, and they inspire me daily. Although New Zealand society is not the most fashionable, I am inspired by how creative and inventive Kiwis are.

How do you develop your garment silhouette?

A large part of my design process is done when I see a garment on the body. I like to make adaptations to a style once I have worked with a first prototype on an actual body. I do not use mannequins for fit, as I find that knitwear comes to life and falls best on a real body. The emotional response I have often helps develop the silhouette.

Can you explain why you produce a northern hemisphere and a southern hemisphere collection each season?

When I launched under my own name I was determined that this label be recognized as an international one. It was therefore important for me to take my collection straight to the northern hemisphere and receive feedback there. The southern hemisphere collections are an edited version of what has been presented to the northern hemisphere. Australasians prefer a darker colour palette, so the southern hemisphere collections feature less colour, particularly for the New Zealand market. Northern hemisphere customers are generally more adventurous and are able to afford more expensive items than our market here, which makes the northern hemisphere of interest.

How do you choose the yarns you work with?

I work with natural fibres as I am just more drawn to them. Nature does such an amazing job creating different fibres for different purposes, and I am also concerned with how man-made fibres impact the environment (although I am seeking alternatives to cotton since its growing and treatment processes have such a high impact). Some of my recent favourite yarns are a New Zealand possum/merino/silk blend and a Peruvian alpaca. The fibre's characteristics make it light and yet extremely warm.

Does your work have any environmental impact, and does it worry you?

I have become more and more conscious of the environmental impact of my trade. Living and working in New Zealand I am unfortunately going to have an environmental impact if I want to get my clothes to those on the other side of the world who want to wear them.

What is the most inspiring piece of knitwear you have seen?

I think Sandra Backlund's work (see p. 184) is quite incredible; not one particular piece comes to mind, but her overall aesthetic is very creative and I appreciate the work that goes into creating each piece by hand.

How can knitwear be modern?

Easily. It is firstly in the design! But I find the pace of technical development in yarns and machinery is presenting some amazing opportunities. I recently saw that Adidas and Nike are now knitting shoes (see p. 7) – surely a very modern take on knitwear? And one of the commercial factories I use knits bullet-proof vests using Kevlar.

Creativity comes from…?

…the heart.

Opposite
The 'When the Sun Goes Down' dress from the 'Armour and ReBelle' collection is made from merino wool. The cable-plait front was created by hand and then hand-stitched to the dress. The 'Happy and Bleeding' stole is New Zealand possum fur.

Left
The main body and sleeves of the 'Concrete Jungle' dress from the 'Eternal Return' collection were knitted with combed cotton. The panel down the centre was hand-crocheted using a mercerized cotton, which gives a slight contrast in surface texture.

Right
The 'Broken Bells' dress was knitted on a commercial 12-gauge machine using mercerized cotton and Lycra. It features the same sleeve detail as the 'Broken Bells' cardigan (see p. 107).

Opposite
The 'Hooting and Howling' collection features small owl motifs knitted from cable detailing and larger hand-macraméd owls that have been applied to sweaters and dresses. This sweater and skirt are knitted in kid mohair. The tassels are individually hand-looped into the skirt.

Lala
Berlin

Leyla Piedayesh was born in Tehran in 1970. She first studied business administration before entering broadcasting as an editor of Designerama at MTV Berlin. In 2003 she began making her own knitted accessories, launching her debut collection Lala Berlin in 2004 at the fashion trade show Premium in Berlin. The label is now sold worldwide in 150 stores and has its own boutiques in Berlin and Copenhagen. Lala Berlin is a symbiosis of urban cool and elegant chic, based on high-quality knitwear incorporating vibrant patterns and striking prints.

The recent 'Quadrophenia' collection explores the conflict between the Mods and Rockers of 1960s Britain and their stance against the establishment, a concept that is embodied in the juxtaposition of masculinity and femininity in each look. This mix of masculine and feminine garments within the collections is a recurring theme for Piedayesh. The layered looks she designs feature easy-to-wear desirable garments.

The Lala Berlin collections are always a rich mix of knit, print and weave with an eclectic combination of textures and patterns.

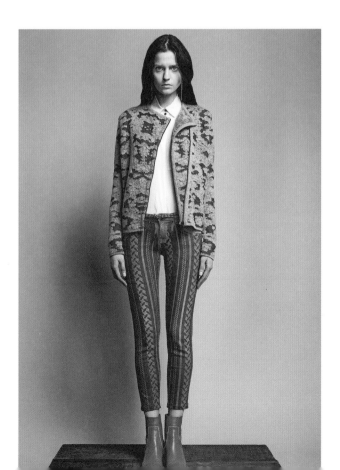

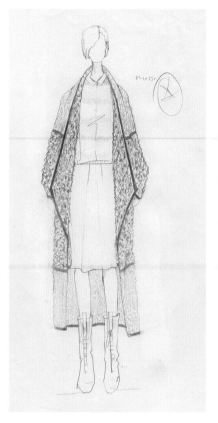

Left
This coat from the 'Quadrophenia' collection is knitted in double-faced jacquard. The pattern of the coat is black with white; the reverse pattern can be seen on the lapel where it is white with black.

Above
Sketch of a coat from the 'Quadrophenia' collection, showing placement of knit across the body and sleeves.

What has been your career path so far?
Business studies – MTV music editor – designer and head of Lala Berlin.

How has your work progressed, season on season?
It has progressed through a better understanding and knowledge of design, material and techniques.

If not fashion, then what?
Nothing else!

What excites you about knitwear?
Materials and yarns – they have so many different attributes and characteristics such as being hairy, flat, thick, thin, soft, stiff, etc.

What other design disciplines influence and inspire you, and why?
Working with techniques and materials, especially concerning prints and the transformation of prints into jacquards.

Colour, texture, pattern, silhouette – which comes first?
It depends entirely on what you are working on, what requirements you have. If you aim to base your collection on a specific colour, then colour comes first. Silk, for instance, takes on colour differently from cashmere. In this case, the dyeing process is most important. It is what you base your collection on that comes first – so, the silhouette and shape, hairy not hairy…

How do you choose the yarns you work with?
I choose yarns mostly according to look and quality. I try to use natural fibres such as cashmere, super kid mohair, angora or superfine merino as much as I can; however, sometimes you need to choose yarn blends or synthetic fibres in order to achieve a certain shape or sculptural outcome.

How important is innovation to you?
Referring to new blends of materials and knitting techniques – innovation is very important.

Craft versus digital – does modern technology help or hinder?
It does help technically. However, from an economic perspective it needs to be seen from two angles. Chain stores profit from technical advancement for mass production. Their prices, however, basically destroy the ability for independent labels to be able to compete. Even though one caters to different market segments, the potential ability for competition diminishes entirely. After all, hand knitting will probably disappear sooner or later, as small-scale production is replaced by large-scale production due to progress in technology.

What is the most inspiring piece of knitwear you have seen?
I guess Sandra Backlund (see p. 184) is one of the most inspiring knitwear designers – her work is more art than knitwear.

Roughly what size is each collection, and how much of it is knitwear?
It is a full collection of ready-to-wear, knitwear as well as accessories, but, of course, since we love knit it is a big portion!

Designing knitwear for spring / summer and autumn / winter requires quite different approaches. How do you tackle this?
In summer it is more difficult to design knitwear as there are fewer yarn options. Therefore technique counts more. In winter everything is possible due to the diversity of the yarns available, and we can be more creative and try out as well as implement different ideas.

How important is the commercial aspect of your work?
We live in the twenty-first century!

Does your work have any environmental impact, and does it worry you?
In relation to other bigger companies or chains, the environmental impact is probably not as striking. However, it is a topic and it does worry me.

Creativity comes from…?
… your daily breath, in and out.

Opposite
Dress featuring a digitally
manipulated, machine-knitted
leaf pattern.

Above
A monochrome
spring/summer look.

Right
Leaf patterns combine with
graphic checks in this sketch.

Laura Theiss

The knitwear of Laura Theiss is strongly influenced by her heritage. She was born and grew up in Lithuania, where hand-made art, knitting and crocheting is very popular. Skills are passed down from generation to generation; Theiss's grandmother and mother were both hobby knitters. Her childhood home was filled with knitted toys, pillows, curtains and pictures, and she made her first piece, a crocheted tablecloth, at seven. She went on to study knitwear design at Central Saint Martins College of Arts and Design in London.

Theiss's collections contain a large proportion of statement crochet pieces. Complicated crochet stitch detailing produces bold patterning in the garments; the negative space formed by the crochet stitches creates the pattern more than the actual yarn. In her latest collection, Theiss has taken traditional knitting techniques and manipulated them on the computer to create unique digital patterns. The patterns were then used to inspire garments in which Theiss hand-crocheted small pieces of fabric and then joined them together, improvising the garment's shape. Sometimes, breaking all the rules of crochet craft, the final effect looks like it could have been machine-crocheted. After creating these beautiful, time-consuming pieces, Theiss wanted to see if the same digital patterns could be used to create knitwear directly. An Italian factory scanned the images and, using high-tech knitwear machinery, produced amazing knitted sweaters in fine merino yarn with the same pattern. The sweaters and dresses are more suited to everyday wear but still have a strong resemblance to the original crochet pattern.

If not fashion, then what?
Art and antiques expert.

What excites you about knitwear?
The best thing about knitwear is that I can design my own fabric, shape and scale just with a simple needle. I can work without patterns or drawings and knit as I go. The results sometimes are unpredictable as knitwear can be worn in many different ways.

What other design disciplines influence and inspire you, and why?
Architecture. There are some parallels between knitwear and architecture, like the clean lines and seams, aesthetics, handcraft and authenticity.

Colour, texture, pattern, silhouette – which comes first?
First comes the inspiration. Each collection has a different inspiration source. Before I start a new collection I try to find some interesting story. After a detailed research I translate it into the knitwear. One season it is an ancient Chinese legend, another early science fiction films and lunar rocks. I am fascinated by Far East countries, people and culture. But always old traditional knitting meets modern shapes. I try to catch the zeitgeist and guess what colour, shape or pattern will be in fashion in one year's time.

How do you choose the yarns you work with?
I like yarns that I can use for both hand knitting and crocheting. My favourite is cashmere and wool yarn mixed with metallic yarn.

Craft versus digital – does modern technology help or hinder?
I think knitwear will get more and more digital. With such enormous technical possibilities and knitwear designer creativity, we will see amazing knitwear in the future. Crochet stitches differ from knitting and can be crafted only by hand, which makes it quite unique, but labour intensive and slow.

What is the most inspiring piece of knitwear you have seen?
I am a great fan of Sandra Backlund's early work (see p. 184).

Roughly what size is each collection, and how much of it is knitwear?
There are 14–18 looks in each collection, all knitwear.

Designing knitwear for spring / summer and autumn / winter requires quite different approaches. How do you tackle this?
Both seasons have their own beauty to design for. For winter I can create long-arm sweaters or thicker dresses. The crochet pattern looks more spectacular made from a thicker yarn. I also can style the looks by layering the garments. Summer knitwear requires more delicate knitting. With a thinner yarn, I spend more time knitting. The crochet looks more like a net. For winter I choose cashmere or wool, and for summer lighter cotton, silk or linen.

How important is the commercial aspect of your work?
I love to create unusual showpieces as they allow me to find innovative ways to knit or display the patterns. I feel free as an artist only if I can knit without any restrictions or consideration of wearability. I tend to work on creative pieces first and simplify a few garments later so the collection is a great mix of creativity and commerce.

Creativity comes from…?
… our daily environment, things that happen around us and our imagination.

Grey crocheted leaf top and
hand-knitted jacquard skirt.
The top was crocheted from the
left side edge, starting with two
stitches and increasing to build
the front.

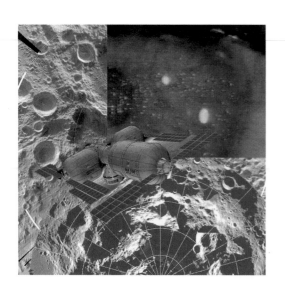

Opposite, top left
A mood board picture for an
autumn / winter collection
inspired by early science-fiction
films, space, the cosmos, maps
of the moon, lunar rocks and
titanium-rich minerals.

Opposite, top right
Computer-drawn design ideas
for the dress opposite.

Opposite, bottom
Theiss's studio, with garments
from the collection in progress.
Pieces were crocheted then
joined on the mannequin to
create a garment.

Right
The crochet pattern of this dress
was manipulated via computer
to create a kaleidoscope
pattern. The pattern was then
crocheted piece by piece using
two yarns: a wool and a metallic.
The metallic yarn was crocheted
over the wool yarn in order
to hide it.

Le Moine Tricote

Opposite
Hand-knitted dress in bamboo
and linen yarns.

Below
The 'Ana' sweater is presented
here as it was conceived: as an
object, a sculpture. It is hand-
knitted in a mix of cotton and
linen yarns.

Alice Lemoîne studied fashion at ESMOD Tokyo but returned to ESMOD Paris to graduate. She gained valuable experience of the fashion industry by interning at Agatha Ruiz de la Prada, Castelbajac, Lacroix haute couture and Gareth Pugh. While still a student, she started working part-time for Rick Owens, and in 2008 Owens's wife, Michèle Lamy, helped Lemoîne sell her first collection of knit under the label Alice Lemoîne. It was a good experience, but she decided instead to dedicate herself to creating a hand-knit collection for the Palais Royal line for Rick Owens. She continued working with Owens until she felt ready to start again on her own, under the name Le Moine Tricote (French for 'The monk knits', a pun on Lemoîne's name with a hat tip to knitwear).

Lemoîne's knitwear is sculpted from modules of knitting that are seamed together to give structure and form. The main modules are usually knitted to create a thick but open mesh that allows the crocheted bands or lacings of the seams to be seen in contrast. The intention is to allow the production process to reveal itself when the garment is worn. Almost all the garments are hand-knitted on 12 mm needles, each piece a complicated, unique patchworked creation. The collections are still relatively small, showing 20–25 pieces in about 15 looks. While Lemoîne used to present only hand knits, she now blends a few woven garments into her collections.

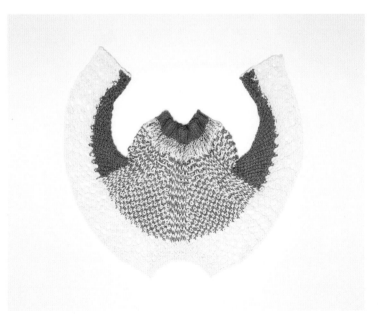

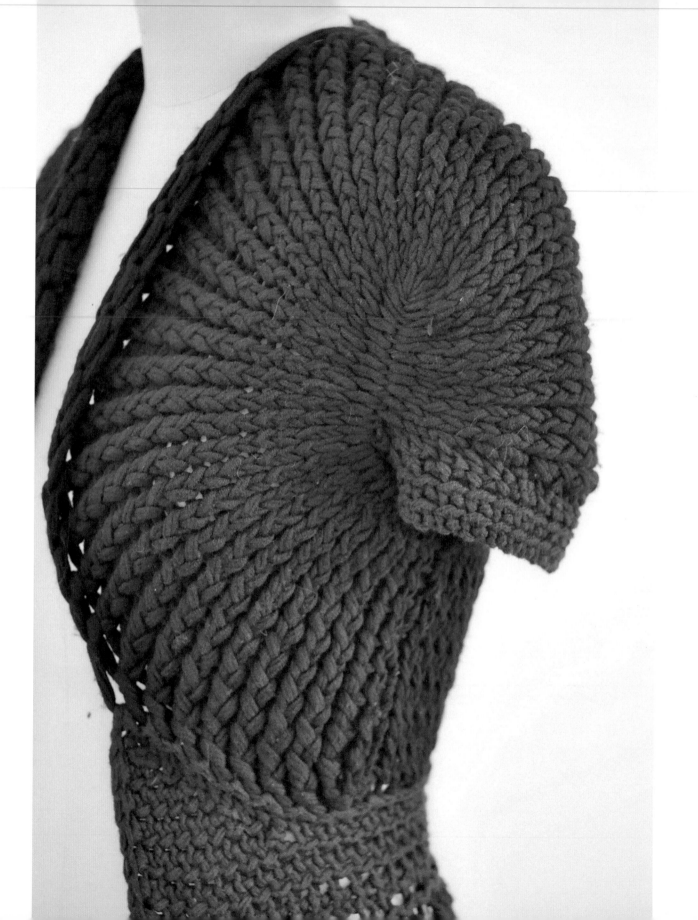

If not fashion then what?
Many things! I would have loved to work directly
with my body, so it could have been acting,
singing or dancing. I am also really interested
in my environment, so I would have liked to
work as an architect or interior designer making
my own furniture.

What excites you about knitwear?
The liberty of creating, and most of all the fact
that there are no rules.

How has your knitwear progressed each season?
Each season I try to clarify my purpose. I keep
the same process of experimentation but it
gets cleaner and more elaborated as my own
technique improves.

**Does where you live and work inspire you,
and why?**
I had the chance as a child to grow up in amazing
homes in Bordeaux, from a gorgeous house
of the eighteenth century to a very contemporary
one (built by Rem Koolhaas). Now I share my
life with Benjamin Paulin, son of Pierre Paulin,
a super designer. So of course I must thank
my environment!

**What other design disciplines influence
and inspire you, and why?**
Interior design for the functional side and
painting and sculpture for their poetry.

**Colour, texture, pattern, silhouette –
which comes first?**
While I am looking for one I find the other...

How do you choose the yarns you work with?
Most of the time I do my own mix and twist
of yarn to match my different needs of softness,
transparency, volume, etc.

**Craft versus digital – does modern technology
help or hinder?**
At this moment I am deeply focused on my
handmade knits (all handmade production!),
but I have always been attracted by machinery.
If one day I have the opportunity, then why not
include modern technology in the collection?

**What is the most inspiring piece of knitwear
you have seen?**
That is very difficult to answer as I can look at
a design and appreciate it for the technique but
not the end result. For example, I adore A-POC
by Issey Miyake (see p. 7) for the concept, but
the design is not exactly what I dream of. My
assistant's mother is also doing great socks!

How do you develop your garment silhouette?
I really enjoy working directly on my mannequin,
so it is perfect to do cardigans and jumpers,
and also dresses and skirts. Sometimes a coat
develops from my research, but no trousers yet.

Are most of the garments fully fashioned?
Yes, all the parts are knitted to a good shape
and size before we assemble them.

**How important is the commercial aspect
of your work?**
Very important. In my atelier I like to experiment
and do some unconventional items, but in the
end I definitely want a garment that has a good
fit and is wearable.

**Do you consider environmental impact when
designing and producing your collections?**
Yes, of course, and this is in my interest also.
Working with close suppliers is better for the
environment but also quicker and cheaper. Using
natural fabric is ecological and also much more
comfortable and nice! (Unfortunately it is also
more expensive, but to me this is a good choice.)

Creativity comes from...?
...intimacy.

Opposite
Stitches spiral from body to
sleeve in this cardigan, made
with a mix of hand knit and
crochet in merino wool.

Left
This long dress mixes hand knit and crochet in bamboo yarn. The variety of stitches cleverly curves around the form of the body.

Below
The 'Acanthe' cardigan is a Le Moine Tricote classic, updated each season. This one is a mix of hand knit and crochet in alpaca.

Above
This spring/summer
collection shows a mix
of hand knit, crochet and
woven techniques, in linen,
cotton and silk yarns.

Right
Detail of the Le Moine
Tricote label.

Leutton
Postle

Opposite
The A/W 13 collection features a pleated jacquard knitted on Stoll machines. This dress is knitted in Lurex yarns.

Right
Mood board for the A/W 13 collection, which plays with bold, asymmetric placement of pattern.

Sam Leutton and Jenny Postle met on a foundation course at Central Saint Martins College of Arts and Design, London (CSM); both continued on to a BA in Textiles, where they specialized in knit. After graduating, Jenny went on to complete an MA in Fashion at CSM, while Sam worked in knitwear innovation in China before returning to London to work as a freelancer. They came together after Jenny's graduate collection was snapped up by Browns Focus in London. The time was right to start something together, as a duo.

The Leutton Postle collections are a beautiful combination of original surface texture with rich pattern in a sophisticated colour palette. Leutton and Postle work with creative craft-based ideas and combine unusual and often labour-intensive techniques and processes: they have experimented, for example, with knitwear and reverse appliqué embroidery, and for a spring/summer collection they e-wrapped over 30 different yarns of varying weights and colours into a viscose knit base. This wrapping technique is very time consuming as it is done by hand along each row of knitting, but it gives a great textural result.

Leutton and Postle's bold designs for both spring/summer and autumn/winter are visually exciting on the catwalk. Recently, the duo have been working hard to translate their ideas into more wearable pieces, developing the silhouette and finish of each garment. They feel they still need to refine this, but the label is maturing from mostly art-like pieces to wearable garments that still reflect their creativity and aesthetic.

If not fashion, then what?
Sam: Sausage maker.
Jenny: Cheese maker.

What excites you about knitwear?
That you can make a fabric from scratch, from one thread, adding, rehashing and designing as you go. Each fabric we make is unique in itself, and this provides a strong starting point for which we are becoming known – pattern, texture, colour. Knit is also a very versatile yet challenging material to work with – it rarely comes out how you initially thought, but this is often a good thing. Happy accidents are commonplace.

Does where you live and work inspire you, and why?
We live where we work and work where we live, which is all-consuming but in a very relaxed and natural way. Life and work merge into one.

What other design disciplines influence and inspire you, and why?
Old crafts such as hand weaving, macramé and patchwork.

Colour, texture, pattern, silhouette – which comes first?
It depends: either colour, pattern or texture, depending on which thing is really grabbing us that season.

How do you choose the yarns you work with?
We have places we visit across the country to source yarns and we use both natural (for feel) and synthetic (for aesthetic). We generally use lighter weights in summer and heavier weights in winter, but there is some crossover.

Craft versus digital – does modern technology help or hinder?
It helps massively. It is important to embrace what is new without forgetting the past. We used to work solely on domestic knitting machines, but now we work a lot with computerized knitting machines. You really can experiment a lot with these and the finish is much more polished.

What is the most inspiring piece of knitwear you have seen?
We aren't usually that inspired by knitwear, but sometimes some really old knitwear pieces can be amazing. We look more at broader textiles, old textiles books where the result is more of an art piece. Other than that, the work that came out of the Bauhaus school is sensational.

How do you describe your style of knit?
Haphazard but planned.

What knit techniques are important in your work currently?
Intarsia and pointelle.

Roughly what size is each collection, and how much of it is knitwear?
The spring/summer 2013 collection was 16 looks, and all but three pairs of trousers were knitted.

How do you develop your garment silhouette?
Just toiling and re-toiling and sketching. It is important for us to find a shape that really works with the knit.

How important is the commercial aspect of your work?
Very! It is important to get that perfect balance between being excited by what you do and someone else wanting to wear it!

How is knitwear evolving?
There are so many knitwear graduates that knit is just growing constantly! Each new wave of students pushes the boundaries more and more. It is amazing to see.

Creativity comes from…?
…us.

Opposite
Leutton Postle took a familiar motif – the face – and represented it in different mediums in this collection. The abstracted face on the trousers was rendered with a reverse appliqué technique. The thicker knobbly yarn on the dress was wrapped in by hand.

Left
Mood board for the S/S 13
collection.

Below
The colourful Leutton Postle
yarn store.

Opposite
The fabrics in the S/S 13
collection were made on fine-
gauge machines that give a
crisp finish to the patterning.
Many of the pieces look like
they are printed, but all have
been knitted. This top (left) was
knitted on a Stoll machine, using
a holding technique in denim,
orange crepe and Lurex yarns.
The skirt and the tassels on the
top have been macraméd, using
Hama Beads; Hama Beads also
create patterning on the shoes
and glasses. This top and skirt
(right) have been knitted using
intarsia in Lurex, crepe, denim
and cotton yarns, trimmed with
macramé and Hama Beads.

Lucas Nascimento

Lucas Nascimento was taught as a young boy how to knit by his mother in Brazil. He came to London in 2001 and enrolled in the BA in Fashion Knitwear at the London College of Fashion. While studying, he interned with British knitwear company Sibling (see p. 190) and freelanced for Basso and Brooke, along with Brazilian designers 2nd Floor and Amapô. Nascimento was invited to start his own label by the Brazilian fashion council and in 2008 showed in Rio. He loved his time in Brazil and learned a lot about the industry and factories but returned to Britain and is now based in London.

In his studio, Nascimento has a 7–14 multi-gauge Stoll knit machine for sampling. It is unusual for a designer of a relatively small brand to have direct access to such an expensive piece of machinery, but it means he can spend hours playing, testing and developing the programs for his amazing technical knit samples before they go into production at the factories. It also gives him complete control of his fabrication, which allows him great design freedom for each collection.

Many of the garments in Nascimento's collections look like they are made from woven fabric, but in fact they are all knitted. His knits often go through various processes and treatments to create fabrics that can be used for every type of garment: for example, bonding a knit to a woven fabric gives it more structure, which enables Nascimento to then cut and tailor a coat or jacket. Innovation in knit through techniques on the digital knitting machine and hand-crafted finishing processes gives the collections wonderful modernity.

If not fashion, then what?

I would be doing something to do with architecture, as I love it.

What influences and inspires you, and why?

London inspires me, the art galleries and people on the street, the mix of cultures, being able to see this on a daily basis. My research is different each season – it depends on what the collection is and my mood at the moment – but I love nature and architecture; I also love art and I like a mix of it all.

Colour, texture, pattern, silhouette – which comes first?

Texture.

How do you develop your garment silhouette?

I have a pattern cutter who works with me to develop the silhouette. As I use so much texture, my silhouette is always clean-lined and sleek. I do not like too much going on at the same time. The length is usually below the knee, and I favour a cocoon shape in the winter.

How do you choose the yarns you work with? What are your favourites?

All the techniques depend on the yarn; that is why I am obsessed with it. I go to Pitti Filati and see what is new on the market. The combination of yarn and technology is what helps to create the new. Sometimes something that is really simple made with an interesting yarn can look very different, or you can use a complicated technique in order to make an ordinary yarn look more expensive and exciting. All my yarns tend to come from Italy (I am half Italian); I like fancy yarns more than silk or cashmere, and I love a blend of yarns. I use synthetics a lot, as they can give more variety.

How do you describe your style of knit?

I use knit in a woven way – a knit that sometimes does not look like knit. It is quite technical, a lot of fine-gauge yarn combinations, something that is quite unique. Not many designers are working in this way.

Roughly what size is each collection, and how much of it is knitwear?

Roughly 45–60 pieces, all knit.

Does your work have any environmental impact, and does it worry you?

I think it affects everything around me and I try to implement it as much as possible, but some things are out of my hands. I use good-quality yarns from Italy, and I am trying to get most of my production done in the UK, using factories in London and Leicester.

Where do you want to go next? What do you want to do next?

I want to establish the label and maybe do some menswear. If I work really hard and am aware of what is going on, I think the brand can become big and be quite important. It all depends on me, really.

Creativity comes from…?

… me.

Opposite
This look is from the label's first salon show at London Fashion Week. The artwork for this graffiti jacquard dress was inspired by the skateboarding subculture of Nascimento's native Brazil. The textural knit fabrication combines the chenille, cashmere and high-tech nylon yarns used throughout the entire collection with a sleek, minimal silhouette.

Above and right
This collection was inspired by
the exchange between softness
and strictness, masculine and
feminine. Delicate, transparent
fabrications were juxtaposed
with harder silhouettes, while the
soft, paler colour combinations
maintained a dreamlike veneer.

Right and below
Nascimento looked to the stars
for inspiration this collection.
He wanted to create a
softness in his knits and also,
through specific yarns, to
achieve a colour that moved.
This ombré-effect jacquard
dress was programmed with a
combination of matt viscose and
metallic yarns that shimmered
throughout the fabrication, like a
shadow eclipsing the body.

Missoni

Missoni is a constant in the world of knitwear, producing season after season of exciting and colourful luxury knitwear that is innovative and wearable. Based in Varese in northern Italy, the company was founded in 1953 by Ottavio 'Tai' Missoni (1921–2013) and Rosita Jelmini after they married. Ottavio was a keen sportsman and represented Italy in athletics in the 1948 Olympic Games in London. He used his knowledge of active sports to start a business designing and producing knitted tracksuits, which were adopted by the Italian athletics team; Rosita's experience came from a second-generation family business of elegant embroidered shawls and fashionable robes-de-chambre. Their individual knowledge of knitwear and womenswear business was a good starting point for their joint fashion venture. Their three children – Vittorio, Luca and Angela – became actively involved as the business expanded and are today managing the family's brand. This strong family connection within the company underpins the brand's strong direction and longevity.

Missoni is one of the most recognisable brands in fashion, with a distinctive style of bold geometric patterns and graphic florals. Within their designs, Missoni often use space dying, a technique in which yarns are dipped in and out of dye baths to give a random colour effect. When knitted in a graphic pattern, especially in combination with other yarns, the space-dyed yarn yields a kaleidoscopically colourful garment. Classic pieces are reinvented each season in wonderful new mixtures of yarns and colours.

Missoni has more recently also applied its aesthetic to interior design with the Missoni Home line. This has been extended to Hotel Missoni, with two locations, in Edinburgh and Kuwait, boldly and colourfully designed and decorated according to the creative vision of Rosita Missoni.

What influence does the Missoni heritage have on the design of each collection?
Colours – we are known for our special use of colour. We always start by creating our own colour palette, even before we think of anything else.

How is the brand developing each season? Are there any new directions?
The business develops as we approach and follow new markets. There is a lot of potential for our Home design collections.

During the design process what other design disciplines influence and inspire you, and why?
Fine arts above all – always an endless field of colourful creative stimuli.

What is the most inspiring piece of knitwear you have seen?
Anything from a fishing net to a hand-knitted shepherd cape.

Colour, texture, pattern, silhouette – which comes first?
That is the right sequence.

Are most of the garments fully fashioned?
Traditionally we cut and sew our knitted and jersey fabrics, although fully fashioning garments today is technically possible, even for the most complex shapes.

Do you have a preference for certain yarns?
We use either natural or artificial fibres but always look for the best quality available. Each kind of fibre has its own peculiar qualities that challenge our creativity.

What are the differences between designing for men and designing for women?
Mostly the choice of the yarn fibres and consequently the 'handle' of the knitted textiles.

What kind of machinery produces the knitwear?
We mostly use flatbed knitting machines. We use different kinds of machines according to our product needs.

What steps are Missoni taking to address environmental issues?
We learned from our parents a very basic ethical approach to work: don't waste good workmanship and always find a way to use your leftovers. There should be no difference between a working environment and a living space. We do our best to follow this philosophy.

How do you see knitwear evolving?
Constantly and surprisingly.

Creativity comes from…?
…being adventurous and not afraid of stirring your own emotions.

Luca Missoni
Director of the Missoni Archive

Opposite
A Japanese anime heroine – a beautiful dreamer who walks and moves in zero gravity – was the inspiration for this summer collection. This look features soft bands of colour within a softly draped complicated three-dimensional knit.

Above and opposite
The lightweight knits in this
collection are layered and
patchworked to create frills and
movement. The dresses in hot
Mediterranean colours express
a carefree bohemian spirit.

Monsieur Lacenaire

Monsieur Lacenaire was a French poet and high-society criminal, sentenced to the guillotine in 1836. Parisian designer Garance Broca's menswear knit label Monsieur Lacenaire expresses the refinement and anti-conformist spirit of this dandy.

Broca started Monsieur Lacenaire in 2011. As a child Broca liked to entertain, clowning around and telling all kinds of stories. This sense of fun and interest in the narrative is now expressed through her designs and in the promotion of her collections each season.

Opposite
This collection was inspired
the work of Hector Guimard,
particularly the subway entrance
he designed in Paris.

Right
This collection is called 'For
the Never-Ending Weekend',
an imaginary hunt that takes
place in the city with fabric
origami animals. The concept
was taken through to the
garments using stylized animal
motifs, obscured like animals
hidden in the wild.

Broca has worked with various artists and designers on projects to promote her collections. These include a short animated film in which knitted garments seem to have a life of their own and artfully move across the screen as the patterns on the garments grow or move, and a 'Sheep Invaders' game on her website that mirrored the motif on a sweater (see p. 150).

Broca often looks to the past when designing. Starting from a classic reference point, such as a pea-coat shape or a Norwegian knit pattern, she tries to make something daring and new, playing with traditional knit techniques, such as cabling and jacquard designs, and reinventing them in her own quirky way. Each season, however, the collections retain their commerciality, as she designs key garments for the male wardrobe.

What has been your career path so far?

During my studies I had many internships in fashion – from the fashion museum archives at the Musée Galliera to design studios such as Chloé and Kenzo. After I graduated, I was hired at Balmain where I was in charge of tracking knitwear, leather goods and collaborations.

Later I had the amazing opportunity to work at Hermès in knitwear development. I travelled a lot during that time to factories and learned a lot about techniques, yarns, stitches, etc. It trained me well in luxury goods.

Soon after, I started working at Joseph, again in knitwear, and I learned more about the business aspect of fashion, especially in terms of prices and margins.

From there I decided that I knew enough to take a chance and start my own line.

How has your work progressed, season on season?

I try to develop two specific aspects of menswear. I like to make pieces in which men will feel handsome, in luxurious fabrics and sleek cuts. In addition, I enjoy exploring creativity with quirky patterns. I like to start with a traditional pattern, such as dogtooth, and then let it digress into a fun, animated version of a video game. I love when a pattern can tell a whole story with one simple image. I try to make my designs come alive.

Colour, texture, pattern, silhouette – which comes first?

That's a tough question. Which came first, the chicken or the egg? My creative process is more about an intense curiosity for everything around me and the images and stories which come to mind – sometimes when I least expect it.

I do follow a path, though, and it starts with choosing a yarn. It is nice to have something in your hand that is so concrete and that you can rub like a little genie lamp. The texture then gives me an idea about the thickness, the weight and, eventually, the general silhouette.

How do you choose the yarns you work with?

Since I worked at Hermès, I have very luxurious taste when it comes to yarn. However, I try to be reasonable and make an effort to find yarn that will be both remarkable and affordable. I also love to try different things, like baby alpaca, which is exceptionally soft and warm. I am not really interested in cashmere since it is everywhere now and tremendously expensive.

What other design disciplines influence and inspire you?

Street and video art inspire me a lot. The stories they tell are not obvious and we come across them in unexpected ways. I like the work of Brad Downey, JR, Blu. I am a huge fan of Banksy. The film that he made about the enigmatic Mr Brainwash and the resulting controversy is to me a new form of art. Fostering confusion and reflection is a master gift. For me, this is what thinking outside the box is all about.

If not fashion, then what?

I am not sure what other art field I would go into, since I have always worked in fashion. I really love to tell stories and surprise people, so maybe film. But in that case, I would be more interested in short films, or little animated clips that are quick and witty, like when you tell someone a joke.

Opposite
This sweater is a double-faced jacquard in merino wool, produced in France. The collection was inspired by gaming, and included a space invaders interactive Facebook game, which was played by more than 18,000 people in one week.

Opposite
The character Monsieur Hulot from a series of Jacques Tati films in the 1950s and 1960s was the inspiration for this picture and cardigan. Monsieur Lacenaire wanted to create a man who imagines his own life. The sweater was knitted in Egyptian cotton, with long fibres for a very soft touch.

Above and left
The Monsieur Lacenaire studio in Paris. The knitted baseball jacket / cardigan on the stand is a prototype for the garment shown opposite. Shelves hold an array of inspirational objects.

Monsieur Lacenaire   153

Nanna van Blaaderen

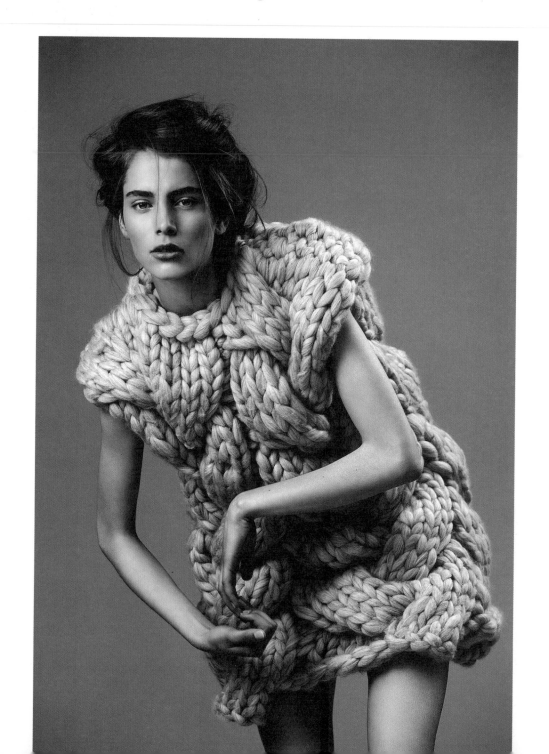

Opposite and below
The 'Dense' collection features oversized garments in which van Blaaderen experiments with hand-knitting techniques in thick, soft merino wool and dense shapes and forms.

Nanna van Blaaderen specializes in tactile, sculptural knitted textiles with subtle structures and textures. Blending craft and innovation, she produces elegant, comfortable and high-quality knitwear. The natural world is a recurring theme in her collections, which favour natural yarns like merino wool, mohair and cashmere. She prefers to work with merino wool because of its refined nature and its soft, skin-friendly and heat-regulating character. The production of her collections is home-sourced in Dutch factories working with Stoll machinery.

Van Blaaderen's fashion education included knitwear design and trend forecasting, and she graduated with a forecasting knit collection. An experimental and research-based designer, she creates textiles that are innovative in terms of both design and manufacture. Blaaderen's love and respect for nature and animal life, together with a strong awareness of sustainability, inspired her to design the textile concept 'Species. A Tribute'. The collection features high-quality merino wool in natural shades of white and expresses the beauty of various animal species. Here she introduces knitted textiles that are a natural alternative to fur.

Collaborations in 2010 and 2011 included Maison Martin Margiela and Maison Celestina Agostino in Paris. The collection 'Species' was shown in the solo exhibition 'Species. A Tribute' at Droog in Amsterdam, and parts of the collection were also exhibited in 'The Making Of' at the Textile Museum in Tilburg.

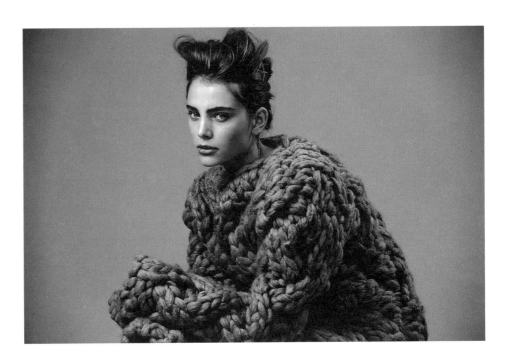

What is the most inspiring piece of knitwear you have seen?

I love the early work of Chanel and Schiaparelli, as they were pioneers. I find them a big inspiration, especially the development of jersey as a top fabric. Liberating the woman, giving her comfortable clothes, it is what I have been striving for – elegant clothes that at the same time are comfortable. I was also inspired by my grandmother's knitting.

Does where you live and work inspire you, and why?

I live in the middle of the countryside with fields of grass, horses and a beautiful river, which really inspires me.

Roughly what size is each collection, and how much of it is knitwear?

I produce a collection of wearable garments each season, but also knit for interiors.

Colour, texture, pattern, silhouette – which comes first?

What I focus on first is the structure story. Then, when this is right, I bring in colour. I work with natural dyed colours; I find them very appealing and gentle to the eye.

How do you develop your garment silhouette?

I tend to have an idea in mind of where I want to go. It is very often clear, simple lines and forms, but it has to be elegant. I start with making the textile, then I get inspired by what garment it could be. I do push it in a certain direction; however, you cannot push a heavy knit in a certain way – it follows its own path. The silhouette is an interplay between what you have in mind and what the fabric lets happen.

Craft versus digital – does modern technology help or hinder?

Factories I work with have machinery for heavy knitting and I research with them to develop ways to combine craft and innovation, how we can create with machines what is possible by hand.

Does your work have any environmental impact, and does it worry you?

As a child I wanted to work for Greenpeace or with textiles. A design path was the right direction for me, but I unconsciously had a wish to produce a product that was inspired by nature but could also contribute to nature. Many of my collections are inspired by nature and animals; the concept 'Species' is actually an alternative to fur because, in three-dimensional structures, it expresses the textures of animal skins like leopard, zebra, snake and reptile. I express the beauty of nature and animals not in colour but in 3D – it is a very subtle expression. I combine nature with my work in a very direct way.

What is the future for knitwear?

There is still a lot being developed in knitwear that is not in the mainstream market yet: for example, whole-garment knitting where you can scan an image and knit it fully fashioned without seams from a knitting machine. Traditional tailored techniques will be pushed away by modern technology. There is also the interesting development of the use of nanotechnology with natural woollen textiles.

A merino wool piece from
the collection 'Dense'. The
hand-knitted collection is
inspired by the interaction
between body and fabric,
protection and vulnerability.

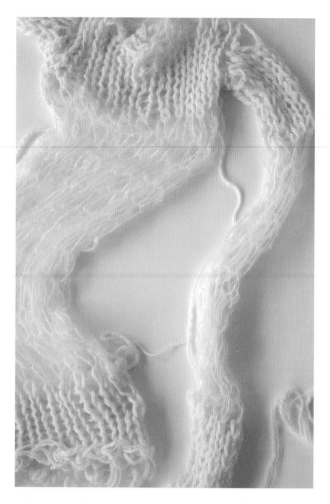

Opposite
The 'Living Species' collection offers a natural alternative to fur. With patterns inspired by African wildlife, the collection consists of sophisticated silhouettes with sober lines and forms.

The collection 'In Movement' is inspired by the power of knitted textiles, with their softness and strength matching the needs of the modern moving way of life, giving warmth, comfort and flexibility. Cashmere dress (above) and detail in wool and cotton (right).

Nikki Gabriel

Opposite
Hand-knitted alpaca / wool
dress with tassel detailing.

Below
In the Construction knitting
patterns created by Nikki
Gabriel, garments are built
from simple, modular
geometric shapes.

When Nikki Gabriel first began her label in Melbourne, Australia, in 2002, she focused on machine-knitting techniques, manufacturing processes and textile technology. Like many designers, she found balancing the conflict between production efficiency and creativity was difficult. Now her garments are almost entirely hand knitted and finished. Her work has developed more as an art practice and process-driven studio, with 20-piece collections and small artisanal production runs.

She is currently expanding her Construction product – a DIY knitting concept for the home knitter developed in 2009 in collaboration with graphic designer and partner Anthony Chiappin. The concept presents knitting patterns in a graphic form based on elementary design principles of interlocking geometric shapes to create a three-dimensional structure. The knitter has the option of progressively adding additional shapes to the pattern, transforming the existing garment into a new one. When Gabriel researched the home knitters' product market, she realized there was a large design-hungry audience who were being ignored, and that the existing product base was largely marketed on nostalgia. She wanted to create something more relevant to contemporary culture, by presenting a new design product that was also easy to make.

Gabriel has recently been commissioned by Australian Country Spinners to design patterns for their Cleckheaton yarn range based on the Construction concept, to be launched in Australia in autumn / winter 2013. She is the author of *The Handknitter's Yarn Guide* and is currently working on a book for her new Construction knitting patterns.

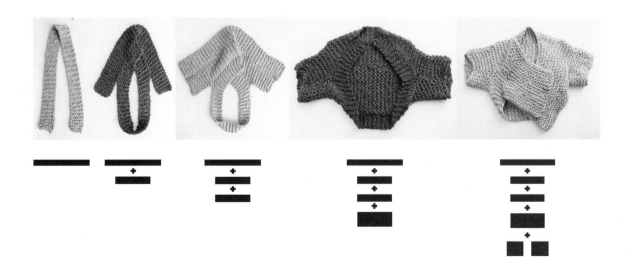

Left
This rainbow of factory fibre waste will be carded, re-spun and recycled into Gabriel's Wooli yarn.

Below left
These hanks of yarn have been hand-dyed at the natural dye lab that Gabriel houses at her retail store Gather.

Below right
Handmade knitting needles by Nikki Gabriel.

Opposite
Wooli recycled yarn developed by Gabriel.

What other design disciplines influence and inspire you, and why?

Bauhaus, because of its influence on the intersection of craft, art and industry, and its modernist, timeless aesthetic. Also graphic design and fashion: I am fascinated by the fusion of new comment and the dialogue of image representation and culture: for example, magazines.

Does where you work inspire you?

I moved to New Zealand in 2010 and have a beautiful studio where I house a collection of tactile things. I am surrounded by design objects, textiles, books and yarns that I have gathered, either to sell in the little retail store called Gather attached to the studio, or just to keep for inspiration in the studio.

How do you choose the yarns you work with?

I have a large archive of knitting yarns on hand that I source inspiration from when I start a new collection. My favourites are the raw, less-processed fibres, such as wild silks and hand-spun wool.

What is the most inspiring piece of knitwear you have seen?

Issey Miyake's A-POC series (see p. 7).

What knit techniques are important in your work currently?

Graduating knit from heavy to fine to exploit drape and form in a fashioned item.

How do you develop your garment silhouette?

I use the drape of the textile to define the silhouette.

Does your work have any environmental impact, and does it worry you?

I practise a 'slow-fashion', low-carbon-footprint production. My studio production evolved to become this, as I was searching for an antithesis to the mass-produced fashion work I briefly experienced early on in my career. I developed my recycled Wooli yarn with a mill in New Zealand. It is spun from a rainbow of waste of wool, alpaca, cashmere, silk and possum, and is not bleached or recoloured, creating an individual quality yarn. Energy use for this production is approximately 80 per cent lower than that used to process fleece for spinning from its raw stage.

Craft versus digital – does modern technology help or hinder?

I work with both. While amazing knitwear can be created with modern technology, the accessibility of this facility is largely dependent on big production and repetition of units. Because the mechanics of hand production are slower, I find more scope to individualize and manipulate design for authenticity for my own label. I make less, and produce for exclusivity.

How can knitwear be modern?

My Construction knitting patterns modernize the idea of home knitting, as they present knitting in a new and exciting package.

With increasing use of technology that apparently disconnects communities, it appears there also exists a parallel movement to reconnect with one another through handmade crafts and group workshops. For generations who have never experienced this community connection, this is a novel and modern concept. I have experienced this directly through the Construction knitting workshops, where there is a great cross-section of people who have a renewed or new interest in knitting through the projects I offer.

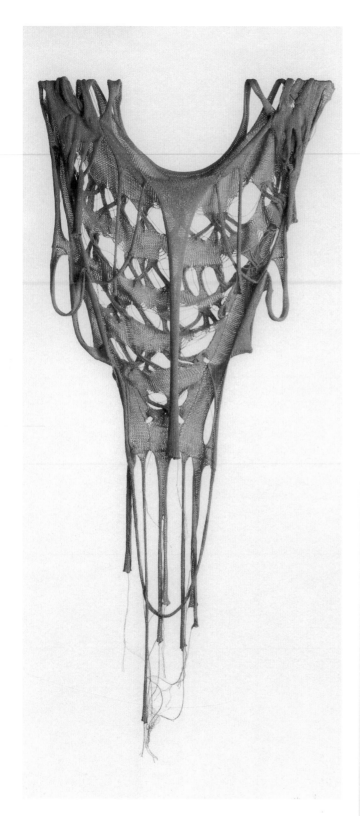

Left
This machine-knitted silk cape was exhibited at 'The Endless Garment: The New Craft of Machine Knitting' exhibition held at RMIT Gallery in Melbourne in February 2012. The exhibition showcased work from 20 international designers.

Below
A combination of machine- and hand-knit techniques were used in this linen dress.

Opposite
A rail of costumes designed for the Australian Ballet for a performance entitled 'Infinity'. The dresses were machine-knitted using fine linen and Lurex.

Ohne Titel

Ohne Titel means 'without a title' in German and is the name given to the New York–based label designed by Alexa Adams and Flora Gill. Adams has always had an interest in visual culture and dress, and was technically trained from a young age by her grandmother. Adams went on to study fashion at Parsons School of Design, New York, in 1999; it was here that she met and became friends with Gill. Adams then spent three years working at Helmut Lang before working with Karl Lagerfeld. After design school, Gill worked at several small companies, gaining hands-on experience in every aspect of knit design. Adams and Gill then worked together at Karl Lagerfeld, where Gill specialized in knit. In 2006 Adams and Gill felt they now had a combination of experience, confidence and a vision of what they wanted their own label to be and founded Ohne Titel.

Sophisticated, directional and bold, Ohne Titel is known for its richly patterned and textured knits that reference the body or play with volume and proportion. Adams and Gill work directly with mills to create their own unique yarn combinations. They prefer to use yarns with a treatment coating or Lycra added, as it gives a stronger and more permanent shape to each garment. This helps them achieve their more architectural shaped garments. Adding Lycra to silk or cotton yarns also gives them a more slick and refined texture, and this can be seen within the collection.

What inspires you, and where do you do your research?

New York is a huge inspiration, and our office is located in the Chelsea gallery district. There is a pulse and vibrancy here that is exciting, and there is always something new to take in. We are surrounded by interesting galleries and new art. After work we go to shows that have ended up inspiring us. Tauba Auerbach's most recent New York show 'Float' acted as the catalyst for our current collection. We also get inspiration from books, movies, news – it all comes together and informs our collections. One inspiration leads to another, like a conversation.

Colour, texture, pattern, silhouette – which comes first?

We first work from an overall visual idea or emotion that defines the season. From that idea, colour, shape, pattern and texture come together and play against each other at the same time. Starting with an overall visual inspiration helps keep the collection focused.

How do you choose the yarns you work with? What are your favourites?

There are some basic versatile yarns that we use over several seasons but in very different ways. One of our favourite yarns is not one that you ever see at yarn fairs – Lycra. We love yarns that already have Lycra, but we also like adding it to stitches to give body or texture. It is sort of the unsung hero, because it is usually invisible to the naked eye.

What excites you about knitwear?

With knitting we can create the shape, texture and pattern of the garment all at the same time. Working directly with technicians and cutting-edge machines, we can reinterpret and mechanize classic knit techniques into modern designs. It allows for freedom in design, if you are willing to get a bit technical.

Craft versus digital – does modern technology help or hinder?

We love the intersection of craft with new technological developments. Rather than focusing on the limitations in mechanization, we like to work with new and surprising results in machinery. We take traditional craft ideas and re-imagine them in futuristic materials or techniques, taking them to a new level.

Does your work have any environmental impact, and does it worry you?

The environmental impact is hard to avoid. We are not willing to sacrifice the quality of the design. It is not our first thought, but we are always interested in seeing low-impact options. The technology to help with this is improving constantly. I think one of the helpful environmental aspects of knits is that the garment is knitted exactly to size, without the wastage of cutting from already-created fabric. I think, in the future, fashion should include more ways to use production processes to recycle and conserve material. Another important aspect of our work is that we make seasonless, non-trend-driven clothing that can last for years. Fast fashion can create huge wastage, and we are committed to the idea of clothing being a perennial object, rather than a throwaway item.

Creativity comes from…?

… courage and freedom to explore. Having a unique perspective.

Opposite
A variety of knit techniques and textures are panelled to create a softly structured silhouette in this jacket, knitted in merino wool.

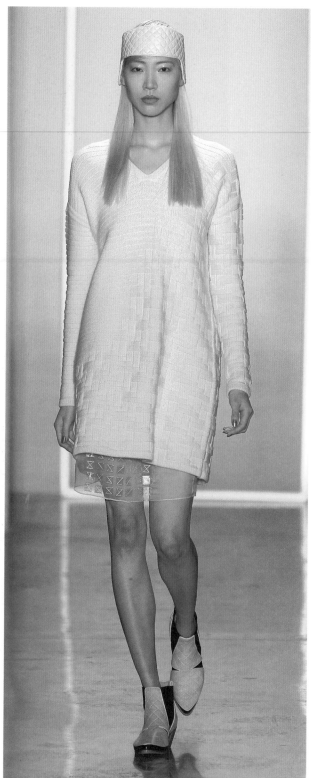

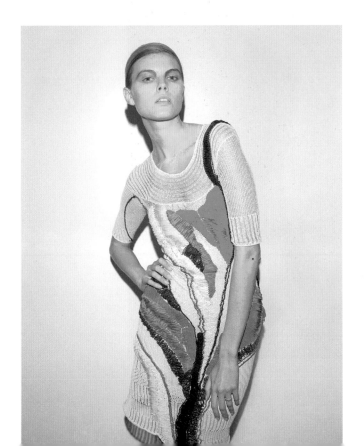

Opposite
This collection played with the
square and rectangle as a motif,
used here for graphic impact
in this asymmetric knitted dress
(left). The square and rectangle
motif used texturally create
a basket-weave effect in this
cream wool knitted dress with
sheer woven underskirt (right).

Above
Graphic navy and white
striped cardigan and sweater
combination in cotton.

Left
Texture, pattern and colour
travel around this dress.

Paolo Errico

Opposite
A layered-up look for summer.
This T-shirt is knitted with bands
of opaque yarn and transparent
nylon yarn.

Above
A laddered stitch works
across the top of this outfit
(left). The same knit stitch has
been applied to the top and
undergarment of this look for a
different effect (right). The body
and sleeves of the garment have
been knitted in one, highlighted
by the horizontal banded stitch.

Born and raised in Genoa, Italy, Paolo Errico currently lives in Milan and
works between London and Paris. After working for luxury brands for many
years, he launched his own label in 2004 and in the same year presented
his first collection in Milan.

Paolo Errico collections have a timeless simplicity, creating modern
and minimal silhouettes in sophisticated fabrications. Creativity, high quality,
functionality and androgyny are what Errico considers to be the brand's
signatures. He designs for 'a Liberal woman', a freethinker who he imagines
would dress in a mix of masculine and feminine styles.

Errico's research returns, each season, to geometric forms like the
circle, triangle and square. They inform a sculptural / architectural approach
to design that looks at volume, balance and scale to create body-conscious
garments. He combines this with an innovative use of materials and colours:
for example, alpaca, mohair, cashmere and wool are mixed with nylon
fluorescent yarn and Lurex to create exciting tactile and visual effects.
A recent collection was inspired by painter Fernand Léger's modern
abstraction, with geometric and sculptural shapes suggesting oversized
volume and blocks of colour from a very specific colour palette. Each of
Errico's collections is part of a constant evolution of the brand; they develop
ever so subtly by a process of fine-tuning rather than extreme change.

What has been your career path so far?

I attended the arts high school in Genoa and then graduated in design with a focus on fashion design at the University of Urbino. My final work was a case study of an industrial design company which helped to develop my very first collection.

I worked at several luxury fashion houses, including Versace, Zegna and Roberto Cavalli, where I experienced a wide variety of different styles. I started my own business in 2004.

If not fashion, then what?

Architecture and interior design.

What excites you about knitwear?

Working with knitwear is always creative and inspirational. Usually I start from a conceptual idea; out of this I can develop ideas for skirts, dresses, tops and coats. Working with yarn gives you plenty of possibilities to design something unexpected and creative.

What other design disciplines influence and inspire you, and why?

Visual and sculptural arts. I take my inspiration from geometrical and sculptural shapes, introducing in each collection new oversized volumes and the 'classic' square, circle and trapezium designs. The hidden and appealing advance of my clothing is front and back wearable items: in this way, garments are multifunctional in terms of usability and personal interpretation.

Colour, texture, pattern, silhouette – which comes first?

Everything comes as one single thing. None is independent but all work together as a microcosm.

How do you choose the yarns you work with?

My favourite choices are organic and biological yarns. I like to enrich them by mixing them together: for instance, cotton with nylon or silk with neoprene.

Craft versus digital – does modern technology help or hinder?

Both are important nowadays. My vision is to create aesthetic designs, which have to be not only cutting-edge but also steeped in respect for traditional craftsmanship and innovative technological advancements.

What is the most inspiring piece of knitwear you have seen?

Alaïa always inspires me.

How do you describe your style of knit?

Minimalism with an eye on details: cutting-edge, urban and refined.

I started working with knitwear as the core to my collections; it was the very first technique. Then over the years I have started to mix knitwear with other garment categories to create total looks. Nowadays my collections are a serene piecing-together of classic 'menswear' looks, crochet yarn, 1970s ladylike concepts and knitwear. My idea is to integrate all those elements in simple, wearable ways that do not scream 'fashion'.

What knit techniques are important in your work currently?

I love to work with as many experimental things as possible. Currently I am working with tricot and intarsia.

Roughly what size is each collection, and how much of it is knitwear?

Each collection has around 60 pieces; knitwear represents at least 80 per cent of the whole collection.

Creativity comes from…?

… architecture (lines and cuts), art (colours and nuances), design (techniques and material) and the people around me (moods and inspirations).

Opposite
A layered and wrapped
monochrome look.

Left
Tonal textured stripes feature
on the back of this cardigan,
finished with a tipped hem.

Below
This wrapped cardigan is knitted
to produce a marled effect.

Above
The neckline of this sweater is tipped in a highlight colour.

Right
A sketch from the autumn/winter collection featured here.

Pringle
of Scotland

Originally knitwear's use was confined to hosiery and underwear, and this is how the brand began in 1815, but Pringle of Scotland was one of the first manufacturers to introduce knitwear as outerwear and this spirit of innovation has not waned. In 2000 the brand launched itself into the luxury arena with a presence in the international fashion calendar in London, Milan and New York.

Pringle's focus is always on high-quality, luxurious, innovative fashion, with knitwear at its heart. In the 1920s, the Pringle signature intarsia argyle pattern was developed and adopted by the Duke of Windsor and the fashionable set of the time. Pringle also took a sporty two-piece cardigan and sweater set from the golf course and redesigned it to create the twinset, which has now become a classic British knitwear style. In 2010 Pringle worked with the Serpentine Gallery in London on an exhibition where artists were asked to design knitwear pieces inspired by the twinset and argyle pattern.

Pringle have developed various projects looking back over their rich archive in collaboration with the MA in Fashion Design and BA in Fashion History and Theory courses at Central Saint Martins, London. Projects have included 'From Hawick to Hollywood: The Women who Wore Pringle' (Pringle was founded in Hawick, Scotland) and 'Princess Grace', an exhibition in Monaco that documented Princess Grace's daily wardrobe, focusing especially on Pringle knitwear. Pringle also collaborated with Sophia Neophitou-Apostolou, stylist and editor of *10* magazine, to design the 'Perfect 10' knitted capsule travel collection. Pringle are constantly developing their brand through innovation in design and self-promotion.

How important is Pringle's heritage to the design of each collection?

The brand's rich heritage is central to every collection, with Pringle of Scotland signatures, such as the iconic argyle pattern and the twinset, always referenced. We have nearly 200 years of history to plumb, and looking through the archive for reference is a huge source of inspiration. In addition to this design inspiration, the brand's founding principles of quality, style, authenticity and innovation are as important today as when the brand was founded in 1815.

What other design disciplines influence and inspire, and why?

We have developed a strong relationship with the contemporary arts and have collaborated with artists including Liam Gillick, David Shrigley, Ryan McGinley and Luke Fowler. These relationships bring a new way of thinking to the creation of knitwear and allow us to work with creatives who bring a fresh and new process towards the creation of knitwear pieces.

Colour, texture, pattern, silhouette – which comes first?

We constantly work on reinterpreting traditional and new stitches, and the texture, weight and tension all contribute to the evolution of the silhouette and colours. Everything works simultaneously, and it is important that a creative process should not be confined by rules and a fixed order.

Do you have a preference for certain yarns?

Cashmere is Pringle's trademark and is always present in the collections – pure cashmere for 12-gauge and chunky knitwear, all made in Scotland, is a key element, especially for the winter season. To achieve a lighter weight, blends of cashmere are also important, with cotton or with silk to achieve extra-light, soft and sheer 18-gauge. A mix of technical fibres plied up or plaited is also investigated every season, to achieve new rounded hand-feel and volumes.

What are the differences between designing for men and designing for women?

Menswear is mainly focused on the evolution of wardrobe staples. Pringle menswear has been exploring new and current ways to approach knitwear as outerwear. Designing womenswear is incredibly creative – it allows for an unlimited experimentation.

Are most of the garments fully fashioned?

Yes, over 95 per cent are fully fashioned, as this is a very important factor in creating high-quality luxury knitwear.

What machinery produces the knitwear, and where?

Primarily Shima Seiki and Stoll knitting machines are used, in Scotland, Europe and the Far East.

Craft versus digital – does modern technology help or hinder?

Modern technology is crucial in moving tradition forward. The brand has always embraced new technologies as a way of pushing knitwear boundaries, and creating new and innovative techniques. That does not mean, however, that traditional craftsmanship is devalued. There is absolutely a place for both in the creation of knitwear and both should be championed.

Opposite
Tilda Swinton wearing a lightweight cashmere/silk sweater. The graphic 'V' shape mimics the diamonds of the signature Pringle argyle.

Left
This argyle-patterned jacket was created using a needle punch technique in wool/cashmere. The sweater seen beneath is a tonal grey argyle in merino/silk, and the trousers are wool jacquard. This autumn/winter collection integrates the brand's signature pieces into a classic wardrobe for the modern man.

Below
An illustration from the Pringle archive shows one of the brand's signature argyle sweaters.

Opposite
These spring/summer sweaters were inspired by Pringle's traditional argyle, which has been abstracted to create contemporary asymmetric patterns.

Sandra Backlund

Sandra Backlund has inspired a generation of designers with her highly innovative, sculptural and beautifully styled knitwear. Backlund works with a three-dimensional collage method by which she develops hand-knitted basic 'bricks' that she multiplies and attaches together until they become a garment. Her knits are always sculptural with strong silhouettes, but although

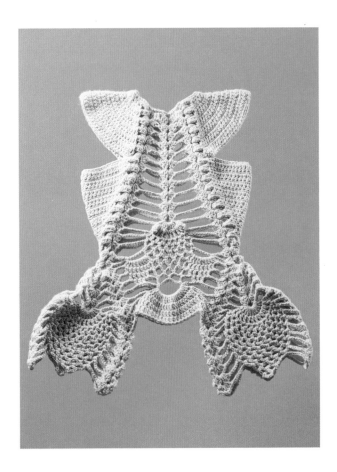

they may look like art pieces, Backlund spends a lot of time on the finish
and fit. When developing a garment, she works with the human body as the
main starting point, improvising on a tailor's dummy, or on herself, to discover
shapes and silhouettes that she could never devise solely in her mind.

Backlund was born in the north of Sweden and moved to Stockholm
to study fashion at Beckmans College of Design. She graduated in 2004
and founded her own company. From the start she made everything by
hand herself, selling made-to-measure pieces directly to customers. For
her autumn/winter 2009 collection, she was introduced to the top Italian
knitwear factories. She wanted to make some pieces inspired by her
handmade collections that needed less manual work. It was a big step
to go from working alone in her studio, inventing the pieces while knitting
them, to suddenly being part of a team of experts within a field of knitwear
that she had not experienced before. Backlund was overwhelmed by all the
possibilities she saw, and though she will continue to create her signature
handmade knits, she now sees new avenues for developing her collections
that she never before thought possible.

Were you a creative child?

I grew up in a rather small and safe city in the north of Sweden and I had a typical late 1970s, early 1980s Swedish childhood with a lot of creative or sporty activities, often outdoors. I have always felt a strong connection to arts and crafts and a need to express myself in a creative way, but alongside the artistic side of me I also have a strong theoretical and mathematical vein. Throughout my life I have had a hard time trying to make these two opposites cooperate. Through the kind of fashion that I do I finally found a way to combine both my free and my computing side.

What other design disciplines influence and inspire you, and why?

I do not look at other design disciplines for direct inspiration, but I use methods that have more in common with a sculptor's, rather than a traditional tailor's, work.

How important is innovation to you?

Not so important. I often recycle my old ideas but try to be aware of any mistakes along the way that can take me beyond what I knew before.

What is the most inspiring piece of knitwear you have seen?

It was in 2008 when I was visiting the Yves Saint Laurent exhibition at the de Young Museum in San Francisco and I discovered his knitted cocoon wedding dress from 1965 (see p. 9).

How important is the commercial aspect of your work?

I often allow myself to lose control and see what happens if I do not think so much about practical things like trends, seasons, wearability and what other people might expect from me. In the end I do this mostly to satisfy myself.

Opposite and right
For the 'Control-C' collection, Backlund worked with Italian knitwear producer Maglificio Miles to make some unique pieces inspired by her hand-made collections but requiring only limited manual work.

Does your work have any environmental impact, and does it worry you?

It is a big responsibility to be working as a designer at this time and very difficult to justify your right to produce new things in a world full of affluence. I like to believe that it is true that we cannot live entirely on vintage things, but also need to be treated with new visions and stories told in the language of our time. What we need to realize, though, is that the main problem today is that there is just too much of everything out there, and that all of us with a mission to create new things have to remember to concentrate on what we are really good at and leave others to do what they do best.

How can knitwear be modern?

I often think about the way some things transcend different trends and times. I do not think there is any kind of recipe for that and I have never noticed anything specific that these garments or objects have in common – that is why timeless things are so fascinating. The same is true of traditional handicraft techniques. I cannot tell you how to use them without being burdened by a classical mindset, or if it is even possible to do that. But I guess one way is to use them more as an inspiration and a starting point than as law.

Opposite and right
For this spring/summer
collection, Backlund was
interested in the use of copper.
She explains: 'With a history of
use that is a least 10,000 years
old, copper is an important
part of both our history and the
future. It's one of the world's
most useful natural resources,
100% recyclable without any
loss of quality, and it's estimated
that 80% of the copper ever
mined is still in use today.'

Above
This piece is a result of a
consulting collaboration with the
Swedish rug company Kasthall.

Sibling

Sibling is a synergistic collaboration between Sid Bryan, Joe Bates and Cozette McCreery, born in 2008 when the three felt there was a massive gap in the market for good men's knitwear. In 2010 the British Fashion Council recognized the brand, offering sponsorship under its NEWGEN MEN initiative. A line of womenswear called Sister by Sibling was launched as a collaboration with Topshop in 2010, and its success prompted the trio to continue Sister as a brand in its own right.

Opposite
The collection 'Darn the Boozer'
is an interpretation of a knitted
pub crawl around the East End
of London. A beer bottle motif
is incorporated in the Fair Isle
pattern of this twinset.

Below
These cashmere twinsets have
been hand-appliquéd with tiny
sequined leopard patches.

Bryan, Bates and McCreery each offer different qualities to the brand. Bryan graduated in menswear knit from the Royal College of Art, London, and began freelancing for Alexander McQueen and Bella Freud, producing iconic chunky hand-knitted showpieces. Since then he has also worked for Lanvin, Giles, Jonathan Saunders, Jasper Conran and Fendi. Bates has worked for various fashion companies including Bodymap and Alexander McQueen and was the head of design at Jaeger for nearly three years. He continues to consult for Jaeger and also for the Jacques Vert group on their high-end womenswear. McCreery has worked for Jasper Conran, Bella Freud, John Galliano and Solange Azagury-Partridge in design assistant, sales and PR capacities. A DJ and all-round social organizer, McCreery also designs with Bryan and Bates. She admits she doesn't knit, but her understanding of contemporary culture and how this affects each collection is invaluable.

The ethos of Sibling and Sister is the traditional that is modernized with contemporary design and humour. They offer the iconic twinset to men in bright coordinating patterns. A classic knitwear garment such as, for example, the V-neck, is redesigned with knitted cheeky text. Traditional stitch details like Fair Isle are interpreted with skulls and graphic shapes or an animal skin pattern in clashing fuchsia and orange. With sequins and sparkle, knobbles and bobbles, every knitted piece is bold and playful in texture or colour more often both.

Each season Sibling work with creatives to push their vision of their collections, whether through short films or highly styled strong catwalk looks. The overall look of the whole collection is equally important as each individually designed beautiful garment.

How do you start the design process?
It can be pretty random. We all have our individual ideas and inspirations, then we come together and it is an amalgam of interests. We all bring different things to the design process. We often start with a character and create a narrative within the collection.

What are the differences between designing for menswear and designing for womenswear?
We borrow and develop ideas from the menswear Sibling collection for the womenswear Sister collection. Sister both shares and diverts from the men's collection shown earlier in the season. Certain motifs might appear in both collections; this season it was Paula Yates's swallow tattoo. For both menswear and womenswear, we work with classic knitwear shapes and modernize them with colour, pattern and texture. We then also work on more extreme shapes where we really challenge the perception of what knitwear can do.

Does where you live and work inspire you, and why?
We work in the East End of London, which is a constant source of inspiration.

How do you choose the yarns you work with? What are your favourites?
We like to work with luxury yarns, natural yarns for comfort and also synthetic yarns that are more innovative and directional. We also choose yarns than can give us great colour.

Do you have any cultural influences?
We are influenced by music and art, alongside youth tribes and street culture.

Craft versus digital – does modern technology help or hinder?
We employ both labour-intensive hand knitting (especially for the chunky knits) and garments made on the latest knitwear machinery. It depends on the yarn and what we are trying to achieve each season. Obviously technology can speed up certain knitting processes, but some techniques can only be achieved by hand.

Roughly what size is each collection, and how much of it is knitwear?
It depends on the styling we do for the show: i.e., scarves, gloves, hats, masks, pom-poms, etc. The last Sister show was 20 looks, which is about a 40-piece selling collection and the rest show pieces. The last Sibling show was 15 looks – about 30 pieces excluding the hand knits and 70ish including (they were all wearing two hats, scarves, mittens and collars).

How do you describe your style of knit?
Traditional knitwear techniques turned on their head. Garments that have a sense of humour and twist to them but that are all ways designed to be worn. Colourful and bold.

Opposite
The femininity of this pink tennis dress from the 'Warrior in Woolworths' collection contrasts with the skull motif on the cardigan, which is knitted with a blister stitch in a viscose and Lurex mix. The outfit is styled with a viscose knitted lace mask and bonnet with paper raffia pom-poms.

Richard Hell and the New Wave punks of New York City were the inspiration behind the collection 'Please Kill Me'. Bold jacquard graphic patterns, fluffy knits and oversized mittens with beanies give impact on the catwalk.

The 'Social Zombie' collection, hand-knitted in Scottish lambswool, was inspired by the SoCal Zombie Walk in LA, monsters, and Scooby Doo.

Sita Murt

Sita Murt has always been interested in textiles. She is the daughter of the owner of a tannery in Igualada, Spain, and as a child would collect small pieces of leather and try to make them into garments. She studied at the Sarrià School of Textile Design, and married the manager of Esteve Aguilera, a knitwear manufacturing company that was founded in 1924. The untimely death of her husband in 1984 brought Murt further into the world of fashion and textiles when she was appointed company manager of Esteve Aguilera. There she worked towards creating the brand Sita Murt. Murt's children are now also involved with the company in different capacities.

A very successful brand, Sita Murt is stocked in 1,700 stores worldwide, with 20 of its own stores in Spain, one in Paris and three franchises. The brand is known for its timeless, classic knitwear, feminine with a modern urban style. The knits tend to be made in natural yarns that give a luxurious quality and feel. As the Sita Murt brand is from the Esteve Aguilera company, it combines design with modern production techniques that are driven by quality and style. Most Sita Murt knitwear is produced on Shima Seiki machines.

When designing, Murt observes the young women she sees on the streets of Barcelona, how they are mixing and layering their clothes in a unique way. She also looks at working women and the needs of their busy daily lives. She strongly believes fashion serves the woman, and not the reverse.

If not fashion, then what?
I am passionate, active, curious…. I can't imagine my life without creation.

What excites you about knitwear?
I love knitwear because it is an absolute creation. Nothing existed before; you choose the yarns, the colours, the way to knit, the gauges – everything! Each garment is a new creation, new research, always starting from zero.

Does where you live and work inspire you, and why?
Being attentive to what happens around us in every detail can be the source of a new collection. My restless personality knows how to interpret trends and adapt this to a style. Our designs are tributes to the tireless woman juggling a thousand things at once, for whom we feel a great respect.

Colour, texture, pattern, silhouette – which comes first?
For me there is not an established order. Colours, patterns, textures come together when you imagine the result of your creation.

How do you choose the yarns you work with?
It depends. Each design is different, and we choose the yarns depending on the garment that we want to create.

The investigation of the fabric is the first step; we do lots of research and when the investigation results convince us, then we start to create. The research process is the most important period and it takes a long time. We always travel a lot and we visit international trade shows specializing in yarns, such as Pitti Filati.

Roughly what size is each collection, and how much of it is knitwear?
Our collections have 200 items approximately, and most of them are knitwear.

How do you develop your garment silhouette?
The first step of the development process is clear-cut: the research. The knit research requires two essential things: imagination and creativity.

Some years ago I had a crazy idea: knitting with wire as a yarn in a machine. Everyone said it was madness! But I was convinced, I wanted to try. We broke the machine needles but finally the result was amazing! Another time a single rectangular-shaped piece was my inspiration. I made two holes in the middle and working on this point I created one of the most recognized Sita Murt pieces.

Are most of the garments fully fashioned?
Yes, whenever the design fits it. We normally choose expensive yarns, so if we use fully fashioned techniques the thread spending is lower.

How important is the commercial aspect of your work?
Very, very important. The commercial aspect in our collections is an aim and always part of our focus.

How is knitwear evolving?
I am a knit 'fan' and I really think that knit is in a good place at this point in time – the best for many years. I hope that the coming years will be better and better.

Creativity comes from…?
…yourself. You are born with creativity, you just need to know how to increase it. As Picasso said: the inspiration always 'catches me working'.

Opposite
This sweater is knitted with an intarsia technique and laying in of yarn. It combines super kid mohair yarn with a soft cable of wool and baby alpaca.

This collection was designed around loose, light sporty shapes in a sophisticated neutral colour palette for summer.

Left to right: A single jersey sweater in linen / viscose contrasted with hand-embroidered metallic sequins; a fully fashioned viscose / linen vest with Lurex; a fully fashioned jumpsuit in viscose and polyamide yarn; a knit top created like a jacquard selection with two colors that work alternately with a tuck stitch.

Somarta

Tamae Hirokawa graduated from Bunka Fashion College in Tokyo
and started working for Issey Miyake, where she stayed for eight years,
becoming the head of knitwear. Although she loved working for Miyake,
Hirokawa wanted to explore other forms of art and design and created
her own company, Soma Design, in 2006. Soma Design works in graphic
design, sound direction and fashion design; Somarta is the fashion
element of the company.

Somarta designs and produces a range of garments but is best known for beautifully engineered bodysuits. Hirokawa wanted to develop a new way of manufacturing and wearing clothes that are close to the body. Garments in the bodywear line, the Skin Series, are not sewn together but crafted three-dimensionally on high-tech knitwear machines, where the beautifully patterned knit and silhouette are created as one. Some of the garments are so intricate in their design that they can take months to complete, featuring handwork and crystals.

Digital technology plays a strong part in not only the manufacture of the garments but also how the garments are presented. Somarta began showing at Japan Fashion Week in 2007, winning the Newcomer's Prize at the Mainichi Fashion Grand Prix. Somarta fashion shows are a spectacle: the catwalk is transformed into another world through the use of creative digital projections. The projections and art direction are developed at Soma Design alongside the garments and help to give each collection a powerful narrative, which is central to Hirokawa and her vision of a new future fashion.

Opposite and left
These two looks are from the debut collection, which was inspired by the book *The Secret Garden* by Frances Hodgson Burnett. The garments feature metallic yarn knitted, tasselled and wrapped around rings for decorative detail.

Left
The age of discovery and
the chamber of curiosities
are themes for this collection.
This long gilet was dyed after
construction to resemble the
surface of coral.

Opposite
This bodysuit with hoof-like feet
has been knitted without seams.

If not fashion, then what?
Some kind of design-related work,
or I'd be an author.

**You are known for your amazing bodysuits.
How did this come about?**
I wanted to create something that was close
to the skin in the most minimal way.

**Does where you live and work inspire you,
and why?**
Yes. I live in Tokyo and there are so many
creative people here, and lots of museums
and lots of culture to encounter.

**Colour, texture, pattern, silhouette –
which comes first?**
Pattern.

Do you have any cultural influences?
Yes. I am very influenced by traditional
Japanese culture and industry, and also
foreign ethnic culture.

**Craft versus digital – does modern technology
help or hinder?**
My DNA for creation is made out of a
combination of modern technology and very
traditional craftsmanship, resulting in a hybrid
outlook. Both are important to me, especially
traditional Japanese craftsmanship, which is
deteriorating. I feel it is my duty to continue
to keep that tradition as a designer.

**Do you look to the past or the future
when designing?**
To create something new, I look to the past;
it is my duty to connect the past and the future.

**What techniques do you use in making
your bodysuits?**
I imagine the three-dimensional shape from the
flat surface of the fabric then start to construct it.

What yarns do you use?
Nylon, polyester, polyurethane.

**How important is the commercial aspect
of your work?**
My main goal is not to make money but
to create clothing that will be part of history.
But I obviously can't keep working as a designer
if I don't make money, and because of that
commercial aspect I can therefore keep being
creative and that is the truth of being a designer.

**Does your work have any environmental impact,
and does it worry you?**
Designing is consuming and against nature,
and to produce something is to have an impact
on the environment. In return I want to feel
I am creating joy and beauty, and that for me
is designing. Therefore, we have to always
appreciate nature and the environment and
keep doing the best work we can.

Creativity comes from…?
…unlimited expanding energy.

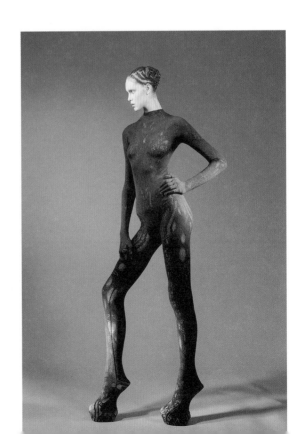

Opposite
This knit has been stretched over a structured undergarment to give a new shape away from the body.

Above
Inspiration for a collection: stills from a film showing the development of life, from cell to bone structure and skin.

Right
This collection was inspired by the nano-world visible through a microscope. The knitted body suit has been hand-embellished with beads and gems to give a kaleidoscopic detailed pattern.

Sonia
Rykiel

Sonia Flis married Sam Rykiel in 1953. With no background in fashion design, she designed her first garments in 1962 when she couldn't find anything good to wear when she was pregnant. Her husband owned a clothes boutique, Laura, in Paris, and using his contacts, she designed and manufactured her popular knitted 'poor boy' sweater and sold it in the boutique. This sweater made the cover of *Elle* magazine, and from that point on Rykiel was known for her knits. She carried on designing for her husband's boutique and opened her own shop on the rue de Grenelle in 1968. Rykiel's womenswear collection soon became a well-known brand as it developed into childrenswear, perfume and homewares and opened boutiques worldwide. In 2007, Rykiel's daughter Nathalie became president of Sonia Rykiel. In 2009 came the first of two collaborations with H&M, a range of lingerie; a collection of iconic knitwear followed in 2010. In 2012, Fung Brands Limited bought 80 per cent of the fashion house and announced a new artistic director, Geraldo da Conceiçao.

Sonia Rykiel remains an iconic knitwear brand. The collections are designed for real women with a sense of fun. The garments are beautifully cut, flattering and very wearable, knitwear designed to be both comfortable and fashionable. The mischievous side of the collections is often expressed through the use of trompe l'oeil collars, pockets and bows on the knitwear, perhaps inspired by one of the most iconic pieces of knitwear, the cravat jumper designed by Elsa Schiaparelli in 1927. Colour palettes are always sophisticated and joyful, often featuring bold stripes. Sonia Rykiel designs, with their patterns and colours, are wonderfully French in style.

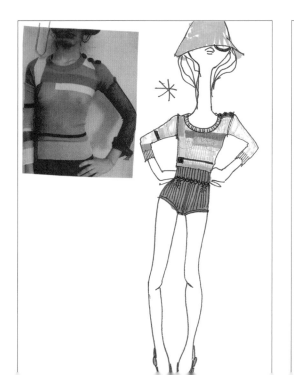

What other design disciplines influence and inspire you, and why?

All disciplines inspire me: painting, sculpture, architecture, everything that is weaved around a block of marble or a lump of stone.

I love to create and invent. Everything touches me. I see differently from others. When a thread interests me, I try to work it in every possible way: I twist it, turn it inside out, wash it, stretch it and iron it several times over.

I don't have any ideas; I create automatically. However, I know that it requires thought and reflection. Before inscribing or drawing colours, I tried, I listed, I assembled hundreds of drafts, I mixed colours, worked with stripes, assembled and enlarged dots.

Also, it's important to find the rhythm of the colours, the right colours, that which makes the collection new and entices people to buy it. The work of the designer is as important as that of the merchant; it's a question of teamwork.

Colour, texture, pattern, silhouette – which comes first?

With everything and nothing, I never know in advance where I will be or how I will feel. I breathe.

This is not work but joy and happiness, though this doesn't mean I don't have sad moments that are hard to deal with. Like everyone else, I question myself.

Do you have a preference for certain yarns?

Yes, I have preferences! Naturally.

What are the differences between designing for men and designing for women?

There is no difference. It's the same, just as difficult.

What is the most inspiring piece of knitwear you have seen?

My first sweater knitted by my mother when I was three years old.

Sonia Rykiel

Opposite, top
In this jacket and skirt, texture and pattern are achieved by mixing a variety of yarns: wool, yack, nylon, cupro and Lurex.

Opposite, bottom
Ultra-fine Sonia Rykiel merino sweater and skirt. The sweater features an asymmetric design with a motif of a skier knitted in intarsia.

Right
This cardigan and dress from the Sonia by Sonia Rykiel line are made from extra-fine wool, which has been used in reverse. The tan and black used in the outfit has been cleverly engineered to create a line from the cuff of the cardigan across the front of the dress.

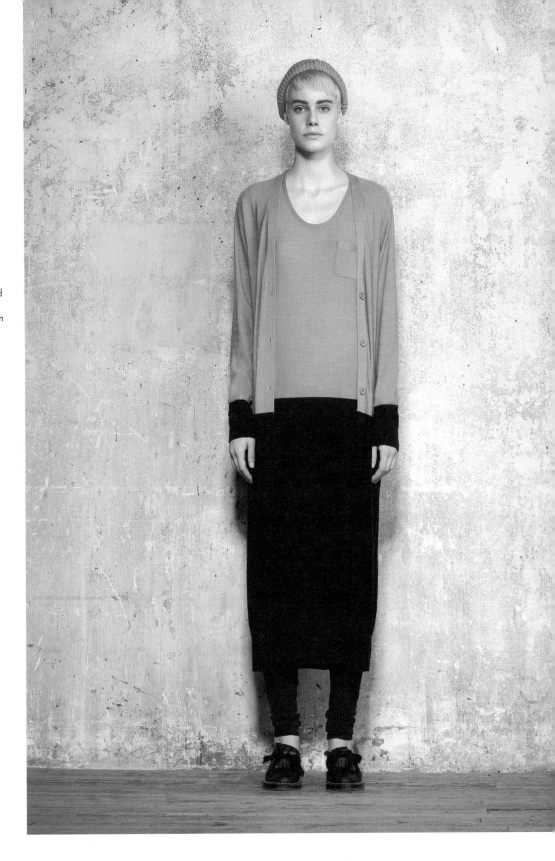

Below
Sonia Rykiel yellow cotton
dress knitted with perforated
ribs and pleats.

Right
Sonia Rykiel cotton playsuit.
The colour blocks are knitted
by intarsia with rib detailing.

This patchwork dress is
created with jacquard panels
in cotton polyamide.

Stine Ladefoged

Stine Ladefoged graduated from the School of Design at the Royal Danish Academy of Fine Arts in 2009. For the first year after graduation she worked as a freelance knitwear designer for a variety of Danish design companies, and in 2010 she started her own label.

Ladefoged is fascinated by architecture and big constructions like bridges, taking her design inspiration from such structures. She is also drawn to darker and mysterious themes, as evident in her photo shoots, in which she likes to tell a story that relates to the inspirations for her collections.

Ladefoged's approach to design has a simplicity found in Scandinavian design traditions. Even though her garments can be very detailed and sculptural, there is still a simplicity in how they are constructed and finished. Silhouettes are bold and pieces are body conscious or oversized and draped in knit or jersey. Thicker knitted and braided panels and strips are then used as details throughout the collections. Ladefoged uses them as finishing at the neck or centre fronts of garments, often contrasted with a lighter knit for the main body. Ladefoged also uses braids graphically to create complicated decorative patterning that works around the body. Supersized, the braids create volume and drama. Sweaters, dresses and cardigans are usually knitted in plain blocks of colour, but more recently she has been developing beautiful intarsia patterned knits that are further decorated with a layer of braiding.

Opposite and right
For the collection 'Eiffel of Bones', Ladefoged took her inspiration from skeletons, skulls and bones. The collection is knitted in merino wool cashmere and brushed baby alpaca. Ladefoged used different techniques such as loops made manually on a domestic knitting machine, jacquard and short-row knit, combining the knit with leather, metal and chains to highlight surfaces and structure.

Below
Mood board for the 'Eiffel of Bones' collection.

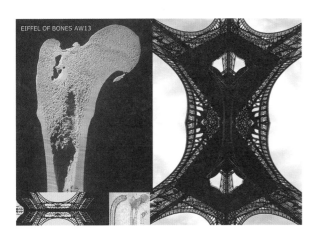

EIFFEL OF BONES AW13

What are you working on at the moment?
At the moment I am working on finishing autumn/winter 2013. I am always thinking of new ways to create and transform knitwear and techniques.

Does where you live and work inspire you, and why?
I live and work in Copenhagen, and I definitely think that my way of designing is somehow influenced by my surroundings. I also believe that my Scandinavian heritage has a great influence on my approach to design.

What excites you about knitwear?
The fact that you can create and shape your own material is very interesting to me. You can decide the shape, structure and volume without the process of cut and sew.

Were you a creative child?
Yes, from a very young age I've always been painting and drawing, and I started making my own clothes when I was 11–12 years old. I remember being fascinated by the fact that I could decide everything about how the clothes should look. I was very particular in what I wanted to make, regarding colour, embellishment, shape, etc.

Colour, texture, pattern, silhouette – which comes first?
It is a difficult question, because they all work together to create the finished look. But I seem to start designing with a combination of knitting technique/texture and silhouette, because the placement of the techniques helps to create and shape the silhouette.

How do you choose the yarns you work with? What are your favourites?
The factories I work with have a large variety of yarn and colours that I can choose from. My absolute favourite is wool; it is the most amazing material to knit and shape.

Craft versus digital – does modern technology help or hinder?
I love the combination of the two. I have great respect for craftsmanship and I am also fascinated by modern technology. It is exactly this combination that can help to create new and innovative forms of expression, and this is actually how I work.

What knit techniques are important in your work currently?
I use a lot of short-row technique, because I love the way it can make the knit three-dimensional. I also use braiding applications and cables, and more and more jacquard styles can also be seen in my collections.

What kind of knit machinery do you use?
I have some domestic Brother knitting machines, both fine and chunky gauge. I use these for showpieces, samples and experimenting with techniques. For production, the factories use Stoll machines.

How do you think knitwear can be modern?
Knitwear can be modern when seen in new contexts that are exempt from old, preconceived ideas that knitting is only for grannies.

Where do you want to go next? What do you want to do next?
I would like my company to grow while maintaining the ability to work and experiment with knitting like I do now. It would also be amazing to collaborate with other companies.

Inspiration comes from…?
…our surroundings, experience and curiosity.

Opposite
The 'Shibari Reflections' collection was inspired by the Japanese knotting technique; there are many references to tying and binding in the knitwear. The garments are made primarily of smooth Pima cotton using short-row knitting combined with cut-out and braid applications.

Opposite
The story of Medusa, with
her hair of snakes, along with
spiders and their webs inspired
the 'Medusa's Web' collection.
This collection is in a darker and
more mysterious direction.

Above
This dress from the 'Medusa's
Web' collection is knitted using
a jacquard technique combined
with braid applications.

Sumyu Li

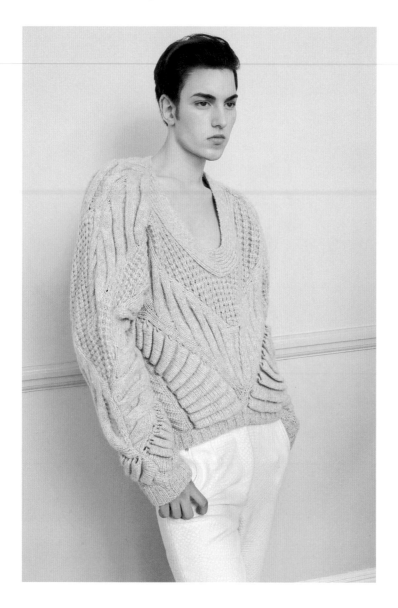

Lola Sumyu Li earned her undergraduate degree from the Hong Kong Polytechnic University, specializing in womenswear and knitwear design. She followed this up by completing a Masters in Fashion Design and Technology, specializing in menswear and knitwear, at the London College of Fashion, graduating in 2011. During her studies, Li interned at Alexander

Opposite
The nude flesh delicately rendered in marble by Italian Neoclassical sculptor Antonio Canova was the inspiration for the collection 'Delicacy in Motion'. In this sweater, gradual changes of stitch width and panelling mimic the male form.

Below
Sketches of outfits from 'Delicacy in Motion', in which Sumyu Li merges classic men's tailoring with machine and hand knit. The first outfit is shown opposite.

McQueen in London and worked with the Australian luxury knit brand Danielle Chiel. In 2012 Li received the Carr Doughty Bursary from the Worshipful Company of Framework Knitters in London for her experimental men's knitwear collection. She also worked on an artistic knitwear project collaborating with the Italian fashion company Zegna and MAXXI, the National Museum of XXI Century Arts in Rome.

Li designs her knits on a domestic knitting machine and combines this with hand-knitting techniques and high-quality craftsmanship. Her garments are technically very complex, incorporating many different stitches to create knitwear with rich visual and tactile qualities, and she is innovative in her combination of knit and woven fabrics in fabrication.

In her latest collections, Li explores the possibilities of collaging with knit and crochet to develop sculptural pieces, pushing the boundaries of creating knitwear in a technical way. She describes her knitwear as sensual, feminine, sophisticated, unique and artistic with a cool attitude. Still a relatively new designer, Sumyu Li is creating excitingly innovative sculptural knitwear and will be an interesting designer to watch.

If not fashion, then what?
An artist! I can see the beauty of an object when nobody else sees it. Being an artist is another way to express oneself, just like fashion. Art and fashion allow people to communicate and give a sense of identity.

Does where you work inspire you?
Yes. I need a clean table with open space to design and draw, but behind my table and where I sit, I collect all the yarns, materials, samples, photos, every little thing that inspired me – and, of course, my archive knit garments.

What fascinates you about knitwear?
The process of creating knitwear fascinates me the most. Creating knitwear is a challenge requiring very strong technical knowledge and plenty of imagination. Knitting is a unique way to create a garment: it is structured from a little dot (loop/stitch), a line (row), then a garment. From the fibre, material and yarn to the stitches, as a knitwear designer, I basically can control every little detail of a knitwear garment, which means I can truly see my ideas come to life.

When I am focused on my knitting I am in my own world. It feels like a miracle and I love it!

Colour, texture, pattern, silhouette – which comes first?
The stitch/texture experiment comes first. I then instantly visualize it with yarns, silhouette and colour in my mind. I think big and freely draw all the possibilities, then think carefully, create samples and do experiments to realize the idea.

How do you choose the yarns you work with? What are your favourites?
I have to touch the yarns and have a feeling for the yarns – there will instantly be an image in my head of what the yarn will look like as a garment. I source yarn when I travel to different countries and trade fairs. Then I make some small samples and experiments to decide if I will use them in garments.

My favourite is merino wool yarn. I love wool and I use a lot in my knit creations. It clearly shows the stitches while maintaining a real softness. I also love working with cashmere and cotton yarns, as I prefer natural fibres. For my new creations, I will explore different novelty yarns.

How do you develop your garment silhouette?
The human body is the main element I use to develop my garment silhouette. I create body-conscious knitwear and imagine a creative yet harmonious silhouette on the body.

What is the most inspiring piece of knitwear you have seen?
Sandra Backlund's knit pieces (see p. 184) – they are very artistic and intriguing.

How is knitwear evolving?
I believe computer-knitting machines will have a bigger role in the knitwear industry in the future. Seamless knitwear technology will replace traditional labour-intensive knitwear production. However, I believe 'knit haute couture' will arise in the high-fashion market, to be distinguished from mass production. While our generation becomes more and more 'computerized', there is still something unique and creative in handmade knitwear that computers cannot replace. People will miss the essence of handmade knitwear.

Creativity comes from…?
…a fearless mind.

Opposite
Machine-knitted wool fabric felted with wool fibre blends into a hand knit in merino wool and angora. The revolutionary hand knit grows as Li gradually changes yarn ends and stitch sizes.

Below
This body-conscious design
utilizes irregular direction and
varying cable stitch widths
with float yarn stitches.

Right
The Beatles' song 'Helter
Skelter' was the inspiration
for the collection 'White Noise'.
Li breaks with traditional
knitting technique and stitch
usage, capturing the mood of
youth culture and rock music. A
striking body-sculpted silhouette
with cable stitch and float yarn
paired with contemporary use of
classic crochet in merino wool,
angora and cashmere.

Above and right
This double-layered sweater
in merino wool showcases Li's
innovative use of cable stitch,
ottoman stitch, rib stitch and
knitting direction manipulation.

TSE

TSE, pronounced 'say', was named after the founder of the company and set up in 1989 in New York as a luxury cashmere womenswear brand. TSE now has offices in both Hong Kong and New York and is seen as a very international brand. The womenswear range now includes wovens as well as knitwear, offering a complete lifestyle collection, and the company has expanded to include TSE Men, tsesay, TSE Home and TSE Baby.

TSE take a modern approach to cashmere, altering the perception that luxury has to be traditional. They have collaborated with many exciting new designers, including Tess Giberson, Richard Chai, Hussein Chalayan, Victor Alfaro, Narciso Rodriguez and, more recently, Jason Wu.

Collections feature a subtle colour palette of beautifully soft cashmere and cashmere-blend yarns in garment shapes that are simple, architectural and modern. TSE combine traditional and cutting-edge technologies, and are constantly experimenting with interesting mixes of stitch and techniques. They are currently developing bonded and coated knitwear. Recently they have been working on bonding knitted and woven fabrics and are experimenting with bonding knit and leather, where the texture of the knit can be seen through the leather surface. Another area of development is applying latex to knits. The design team are currently working with reversible garments within the collection, offering the option of wearing these fabrics either way.

What other design disciplines influence and inspire you, and why?

The biggest influences do not really come from fashion, they come from architecture and interior design, pieces of industrial design and graphic design, so we are really being inspired by what is going on around us.

Colour, texture, pattern, silhouette – which comes first?

Colour does not come first. Sometimes it starts from the stitch and this dictates the silhouette you can make from that stitch, and sometimes it comes from the silhouette and then we back into the stitch.

Do you have a preference for certain yarns?

TSE is known for cashmere so this is the main yarn that we focus on. It may be 100 per cent cashmere or a blend. It can be as fine as a 2/80s yarn or it can go to a really thick chainette yarn that can only be hand-knitted.

How do you develop the garment silhouette?

We work draping on the stand for more complicated styles and also with flat patterns. Some garments we simply spec out – when we work with factories we will send them a drawing with very detailed measurements.

What are the differences between designing for men and designing for women?

The men's and women's collections are closely connected when we design. We use the same yarns, and some of the stitches even translate into both menswear and womenswear.

Craft versus digital – does modern technology help or hinder?

It definitely helps the process. Craft and technology nowadays go hand in hand; when we think of craft, we think of handmade or hand-knitted. It is important that a collection is balanced between the two, craft and digital.

What is great about the machines and technology, like the Shima, is that you can easily create a jumper in one piece without any seams, which is really incredible; however, technology is not going to win over craft knitting. There are still quite a few things that you cannot do on machines. There are stitches that cannot be done: for example, the circle stitch that we developed for autumn 2013.

What kind of machinery produces the knitwear?

We do not have machines in the studio, but we have access to amazing facilities in our offices in Hong Kong and we can get swatches made really quickly. Sometimes we send a photo or texture, maybe nothing to do with knit. Sometimes it can be an old out-of-print knit book from Amazon that has a cool stitch from the 1920s which we modernize and update, trying it in different gauges or yarns.

Opposite
The plain top and sleeves in this cotton resort dress contrast with the ribbed lower section.

A study of the character and qualities of decorative glass from the nineteenth and early twentieth century inspired one autumn/winter collection. Key stitches (left) and devoré patterns (right) create variations of texture and echo the elegant facets and bevels of period glassware.

Left
This cashmere sweater has been knitted using a bobble stitch. The skirt has been patterned to mimic the alternating transparency and opacity of bevelled glass using a devoré technique, in which the fabric is partially dissolved by a chemical gel.

Below
Detail of bobble stitch.

Walter Van Beirendonck

Belgium-born Walter Van Beirendonck studied fashion at the Royal Academy of Fine Arts in Antwerp and is known as one of the radical new designers of the 'Antwerp Six', along with Dirk Van Saene, Dries Van Noten, Dirk Bikkembergs, Ann Demeulemeester and Marina Yee. Van Beirendonck started his own company in 1983. With his interest in technology, he was one of the first designers to create a website for his label – an interactive site that showed his collections, computer games and product information. He has been teaching in the Fashion Department of the Royal Academy of Arts, Antwerp, since 1985 and in 2006 became head of the department, a job that he loves.

In addition to seasonal fashion collections, Van Beirendonck has designed costumes for film, ballet and theatre, as well as for the band U2's PopMart tour. He has also designed commercial fashion lines, including childrenswear, rainwear and worker outfits for city cleaners and garden caretakers for the municipality of Antwerp. He has curated exhibitions, illustrated books and designed various products. Van Beirendonck is an intelligent, inquisitive designer who enjoys developing his ideas across many design disciplines. The extra design work that he undertakes, as well as feeding his curiosity, gives him the financial stability to have greater freedom of design in his own fashion line, allowing him to experiment and push boundaries with less commercial constraint. He keeps his business small, enabling him to be very hands-on in the design process and to make the day-to-day decisions that are needed for each collection.

The Walter Van Beirendonck label has a strong image, bold, humorous and a bit naughty. Interesting textiles and knitwear play a leading role in each collection. Each season Van Beirendonck experiments with techniques and fabrications, mixing textures within strong silhouettes, more often in a bright colour palette. The narrative within the collection is very important to Van Beirendonck, often expressed through graphic slogan statements on garments and catwalk styling. He likes to address big issues, but however important the story or message, he tries to keep the overall concept of the collection positive and up-beat.

Opposite
The wonderful colour palette within this sweater, from the collection 'Shut Your Eyes to See', is achieved through a combination of cotton, wool and special Japanese yarns with some touches of French Lurex.

If not fashion, then what?
Nature and animals. Art and travelling.

What excites you about knitwear?
The flexibility of the yarn. The possibility to create patterns. The possibility to be creative.

Does where you live and work inspire you, and why?
The world inspires me. Antwerp is the place where I write / draw / design my stories and collections.

How do you describe your style of knit?
Adventurous, colourful, fresh and bright, daring.

Where do you find your research for each collection?
Depending on my actual interests, I start up with research in different fields and directions. Anything and any image / impression can be a start for an idea: books, travel and visits, museums and galleries, movies and music, the web....

Colour, texture, pattern, silhouette – which comes first?
Colour first, than the rest together. I am deciding this during my sketching period.

How do you develop your garment silhouette?
By sketching the complete looks and silhouette.

How much of your collections is knit?
In winter, knit plays an important role in the collection.

Craft versus digital – does modern technology help or hinder?
I always mixed craft and digital. I love intarsia (hand) techniques, but I also work with the most advanced machines.

What knit techniques are important in your work currently?
Hand-knit intarsia.

How do you choose the yarns you work with? What are your favourites?
I love mohair and mixed / melé yarns at the moment.

What kind of machinery do you use for sampling and production?
No idea. The manufacturer realizes my ideas on any machine necessary.

How can knitwear be seen as modern?
Just watch my collections!

Creativity comes from…?
…the guts, brain and hands.

Right
The pattern in this sweater from the 'Lust Never Sleeps' collection is created with combination of wool and brushed mohair.

Opposite
Hand-knitted in Italy, this sweater from the 'Shut Your Eyes to See' collection features an asymmetrical design and tassel details.

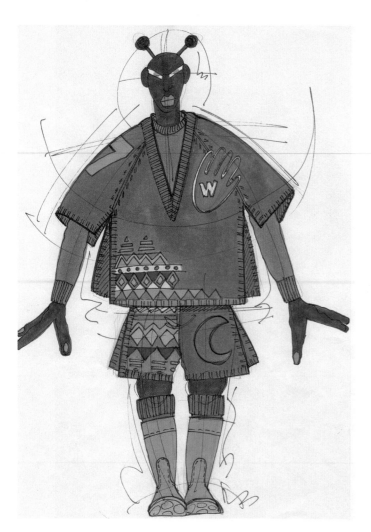

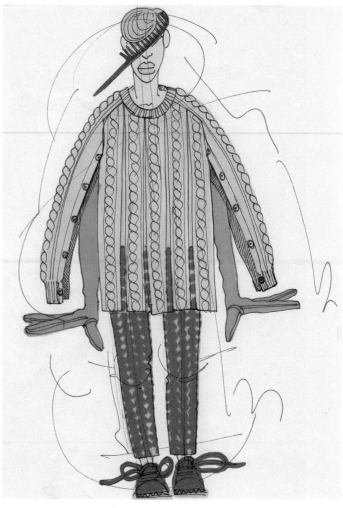

Above
Illustrations for the 'Hand on
Heart' collection (left) and
'Cloud No. 9' collection (right).

Opposite, left
Wool and mohair are combined
in this sweater from the 'Lust
Never Sleeps' collection.

Opposite, right
Knitted from Japanese yarns,
this sweater from the 'Hand
on Heart' collection features
a button-through side opening
detail from the sleeve cuff
to the hem. When the sleeves
are opened, the sweater
transforms into a poncho.

Xavier Brisoux

Xavier Brisoux's knitwear is beautifully poetic, showing a wonderful sensitivity to yarn and stitch. His exquisite knits are wearable and commercial, yet unique. Working mainly in a neutral colour palette of creams, black, greys and blues, they have a classic feel but are thoroughly modern.

Graduating with a Masters in Fashion Knitwear from Central Saint Martins College of Arts and Design in 2005, Brisoux worked with Anne Valérie Hash before starting his own label in 2006. Brisoux says he works

with patterns; however, these are not the usual Fair Isle and jacquard patterns associated with knitwear, but rather the subtle interplay of textures and tones and their placement in the garment. These patterns are created by juxtaposing a lightweight yarn with something heavier, a matt finish with shine, or transparency with opacity. Each of his collections has a strong concept with a narrative. In a collection entitled 'Ab sens', he used a nylon transparent yarn that allowed him to create patterns in the knit that evoked other garments that were not actually there. Another narrative Brisoux works with is 'unicity and duality'; here he experiments with merging two jumpers into one. Brisoux also likes to work flaws into the knits, using mismatched lengths, laddered knit and gauge changes to create an overly tight knit or too loose a construction in a knit piece.

Living and working in Lille, France, Brisoux initially designed men's knitwear but he now also produces a strong womenswear line. Each season has 25 – 30 designs. For autumn / winter 2010 he worked with Topshop to produce a collection for their new Emerge range by contemporary new designers.

What excites you about knitwear?

The fact that it is infinite. With knitwear you can create very differently from woven fabric. You can reinvent the whole structure of a garment: where the seams are, get rid of them; sculpt your whole design in one piece without seams. That is the core of my research.

How do you describe your style of knit?

I would describe it as a reinvention of classic knitwear codes. With every collection comes a concept, and I am always looking at knit classics and how I can express them in a new way through the theme of the season.

How has your work progressed, season on season?

My work keeps evolving each season as I am trying to push the technical aspects of knitwear. I have witnessed a return to smaller-scale production, which frees me to experiment on techniques that are not necessarily mass producible. This means that I am able to have designs that can be completely produced on domestic knitting machines. I have been experimenting a lot with partial knitting lately, and this has allowed me to really sculpt my pieces, while questioning the cut and shapes of knitted pieces.

Does where you live and work inspire you, and why?

I can create anywhere, and, in that sense, where I live has little influence on me. However, there is one thing I need: solitude. The act of designing is a very selfish one, and I cannot create when surrounded. I need to have my 'bubble' around me, protecting me from the outside world and helping me focus on what I am trying to say with the current collection.

Do you look to the past or the future when designing?

I guess both are important. I usually look only towards the future, because I am a fervent believer that the best is always yet to come. But, for me, acknowledging what has been done before is very important in order to not repeat it, but to build from it and reinvent.

Do you enjoy the different requirements of designing for spring/summer and autumn/winter?

I find that question very interesting. When I started my own label, designing for spring was harder. Nowadays, I see each collection as a story I tell, so I look at spring/summer the same way I envision autumn/winter.

How important is the commercial aspect of your work?

Even if it does not come into the early stages of imagining the collection, it is my primary concern when it comes to designing the garments. Each piece should be wearable. Even if it is only for special occasions, at the end of the day we are producing garments to be worn, not pieces of art. I love the quote from Pierre Bergé, Yves Saint Laurent's partner, who said: 'Fashion is tricky because it is not art but you have to be an artist to make it.'

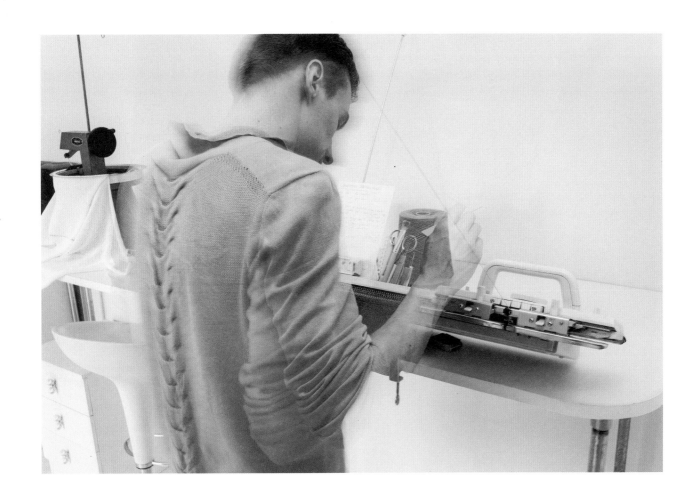

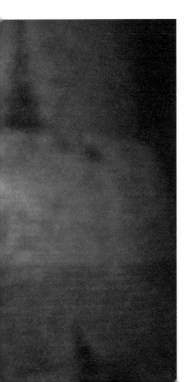

Above
Brisoux in his studio in Lille, northern France. He wears a jumper from his collection 'Fil-amant', a pun on the words 'filament' and 'thread-lover'. The back spine detail is created by lifting stitches up and sideways within the knit.

Left
The 'Fil-amant' collection focused on the fragility of life, a theme echoed in this delicate sweater constructed from a cotton crêpe yarn. The front of the garment is connected to the sleeves by a yarn braided on a linker machine, which is normally used to join the seams of knitted garments.

Xavier Brisoux   241

Above
Knitted on a Shima machine,
the transparent nylon back of
this garment forms the shape
of a tank top.

Left
Sketch of a design from
the winter 'Reminaissance'
collection. The inspiration
behind the collection was skin
change, hence the double
sweater falling at the back.
A second set of sleeves are
knotted at the bust.

Right
Everything hangs by
a thread in the 'Fil-amant'
collection. This design detail
expresses the fragility that
inspired the collection.

Below
A sweater made with two pairs
of sleeves, one cotton and one
transparent nylon, with the arm
sandwiched between the two.

Yang Du

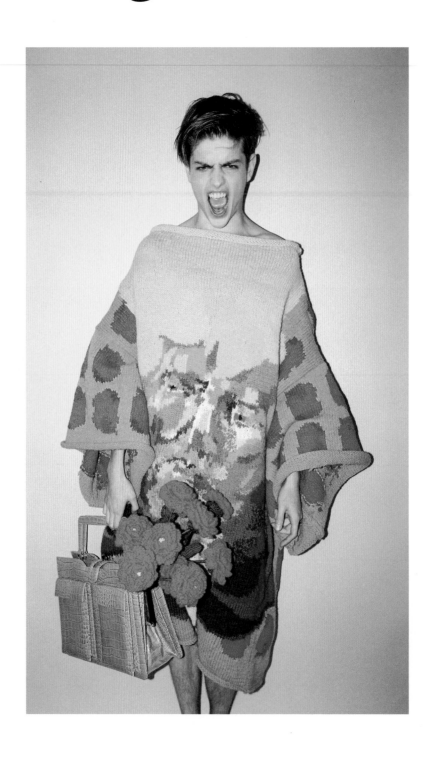

Yang Du completed a BA in Fashion Design for Print then went on to an MA in Womenswear at Central Saint Martins in London. While designing her final collection, Yang Du became interested in knit in quite an unusual way: she was trying to translate a drawing she had done of some raw meat into a textile and could not get the feeling she wanted through print or embroidery. She eventually found that crochet best described it, and she created a fabric that became a dress. She realized that crochet and knit could give her texture and also a new luxury that her printed garments had not so far delivered. By knitting her images she is not translating her artworks so literally, which gives her designs more interest and the collection more depth. The collection now features knitted garments in the winter, but in the summer she still uses print and embroidery on both jersey and woven garments.

Each collection has a strong narrative inspired by Yang Du's life, the places she has visited and the people she has met. Animal imagery is represented with a human character that tells a story, with all the individual pieces having their own identity. Many fashion designers create garments working on a stand to develop a silhouette and detail; Yang Du develops hers through characters.

The 'Buda and Past' collection was inspired by a trip to a food market in Egypt. These two garments are hand-knitted in wool. Yang Du has created a painterly effect by combining a rich variety of colours in the faces.

These two oversized sweaters are hand-knitted intarsia in cashmere. The artwork is engineered to fill the garment shape, travelling across and around the body and down the sleeves.

How do you describe your style of knit?
Luxury, handcrafted, in a sense old-fashioned. Relaxed, sexy but not contrived. I like a relaxed teenage look, not body conscious.

What has been your career path so far?
Finalist at International Talent Support #7; winner of NEWGEN, spring/summer 2011.

If not fashion, then what?
Music.

What excites you about knitwear?
I like the way different media can translate my images, and different yarns can build up texture and shape. It is an emotional process of making and loving something that you are so proud of creating.

Does where you live and work inspire you, and why?
I have been living in London for the last 10 years, and I have travelled a lot as well. I am inspired by the places I have been, the people I have met and the stories I like to share.

What other design disciplines influence and inspire you, and why?
I am inspired by music, art, film, design, everything around me. I love the book called *Art to Wear* by Julie Schafler Dale.

Colour, texture, pattern, silhouette – which comes first?
The story. Imagery is also very important – I am a very visual person and what I see really inspires me. I am very sensitive with the visual image.

How do you choose the yarns you work with?
Quality and texture, what I want to say with the piece, and how people feel when they wear it.

How much knit is in each collection?
I do less knit for summer. I might use knit for a hand-knit accessory or hat. For spring/summer I use cotton and silk jersey and wovens mixed; it depends on the design I am working with and the texture I want. The fabrics have to reflect the character of the image. For example, if I am representing a crocodile, I might use silk satin for the teeth, and maybe cotton fabric for the rest.

The garments in jersey and woven garments are patchworked together with some detail appliquéd on or printed. The knitwear is intarsia, hand and machine.

How do you develop your garment silhouette?
For the graphic work I need a big canvas to play with, so an oversized shape works for me. The mini dress is sweet and cool too, it really just depends on the design I am trying to translate. For example, if I am designing a giraffe pattern dress then I need a long dress rather than an oversized one. I am always thinking about my design first, and then I find the solution. It takes time to work the dresses out. All the seams have to match with the patchworked pieces of imagery to make it perfect on the body.

How important is the commercial aspect of your work?
I have to think of the commercial aspect: for example, colour. In America they like a purplish pink colourway from me, and also my customers there are slightly older – aged 40–60 – and I have to think of this. It is more than just designing.

Creativity comes from…?
…being yourself.

Opposite
Noah's ark was the inspiration
for this collection, full of large
graphic animal heads hand-
knitted into dresses.

Above
Graphic design for the
front of the elephant dress
shown in the look opposite.
The colours were changed
in the final garment.

Left
This cashmere dress
demonstrates a playful
use of scale and colour.

Knit terminology

TECHNIQUES

Knitting
A knitted fabric is constructed from a length of yarn that is looped to create a series of connections. The size of the needles, the thickness and type of yarn and the type of stitch used can create a variety of thicknesses, textures and patterns.

Hand knitting
This is usually created on a pair of needles, but more needles can be used to allow for colour changes and the addition of extra yarn to create textures. Knitting can be created on broom handles, fingers or even arms to create big, chunky knits.

Partial knitting
Needles are selected so that some stitches are held and others are knitted, so increasing and decreasing stitches in the knit, which creates shape. Flare, darts, necklines and armholes can be created in this way, or it can be used for decorative effect.

Tension or gauge
The tension is the number of stitches or rows in a measured area. Too few stitches will make the knit too loose and the resulting garment too big; too many stitches will create a fabric that is too tight and the garment will be too small.

Crochet
Crochet begins with one length of yarn. After knotting the yarn to a crochet hook, each stitch is looped back through the previous stitch, forming a chain. Using the hook, stitches are then added to the chain by pulling loops of yarn through each loop of the chain to create a fabric. Crochet creates an open structure, with the negative spaces creating patterns. Texture can be created by wrapping yarn around the hook while looping or by looping on top of existing stitches.

Macramé
In this technique, yarn is knotted to create a decorative textured fabric. No tools are needed to construct macramé.

STITCHES

Cable knit
Groups of stitches are transferred across the knitted surface creating a raised twisted cable.

Inlay and wrapping
Yarn is laid onto the surface of the knit or wrapped around the needles of the machine and is then knitted into the fabric as the base-fabric stitches catch it down. Yarns that would normally be too thick, too thin or maybe too textured to knit with can be incorporated into a knit using this method. Fringing and looping can also be created in this way

Lace stitch
A stitch is transferred from the needle it should go onto next to a different needle, which creates a controlled hole as the knitting continues. Laddered effects and intricate lace patterns can be developed in this way.

Slip or float stitch
Yarn is knitted, then floats or travels across the back of the knit while another yarn is used, then is incorporated back into the knit. This technique can be used to create patterns or to change colour: Fair Isle and jacquard are examples. The floats are usually found on the back of the knit, but they can be used decoratively at the front.

Tuck stitch
A stitch or stitches are held on the needle while the rest of the piece continues to be knitted – this results in a pulled or tucked effect. This can create a bubbled or indented look, depending on which side of the fabric is used.

Rib
A rib is created by knitting alternate columns of knit and purl stitch.

PATTERNS

Fair Isle
A traditional style of pattern originating from the Fair Isle, an island between Orkney and Shetland.

Intarsia
A method of using multiple colours of yarn across a row with no untidy float stitches. The pattern on the back is as neat as the front of the fabric.

Jacquard

A pattern that is created using more than one yarn (see Slip or float stitch). On industrial knitting machines, the floats are knitted in on a jacquard pattern to produce a double-sided knit fabric.

KNIT FABRICS

Jersey

Jersey is normally a flat fabrication knitted in a length or tube; garments are then constructed using the cut and sew process.

PRODUCTION METHODS

Cut and sew

The knitted garment is cut from a length of knitted fabric and then sewn together.

Fully fashioned knitwear

The knit is shaped as it is crafted, ready to be joined together to create a garment. This gives a high-quality finish to a knitted garment. Fully fashioned garments are created through partial knitting techniques (see Partial knitting).

3D knitting

Garments are knitted three-dimensionally, so few or no seams are needed.

MACHINES

Single-bed machines

These knitting machines have one flat bed of needles all working in the same direction. Machines that work with fine to medium yarn are known as 'fine gauge', with 250 needles across the bed. A standard gauge contains 200 needles, while a chunky gauge contains 100 needles and is ideal for thicker yarns.

Double-bed machines

Double-bed or V-bed knitting machines have two sets of needles set opposite each other and produce double-knit or rib fabric. Dubied is a brand of industrial hand-operated machine.

Electronic industrial machines

These machines can knit more quickly than domestic machines. Designs can be developed on the computer for production. Machines can knit and construct garments simultaneously, with few or no seams. Circular knitting machines produce a continuous tube of knitting. Stoll, Shima Seiki and Protti are brands of electronic knitting machine.

Contacts

Allude
www.allude-cashmere.com

Brooke Roberts
www.brookeroberts.net

Camilla Bruerberg
www.camillabruerberg.com

Christian Wijnants
www.christianwijnants.be

Daniel Palillo
danielpalillo.net

Eleanor Amoroso
eleanoramoroso.com

Escorpion
escorpion.com

ESK
www.eskcashmere.com

FUTURE CLASSICS©
www.futureclassicsfashion.com

Gaia Brandt
gaiabrandt.com

Gary Bigeni
www.garybigeni.com

Iris von Arnim
www.irisvonarnim.de

James Long
www.jameslonguk.com

Johan Ku
www.johanku.com

Julia Ramsey
juliaramseyknitwear.com

Julien Macdonald
julienmacdonald.com

Kylee Davis
kyleedavis.com

Lala Berlin
www.lalaberlin.com

Laura Theiss
www.lauratheiss.com

Le Moine Tricote
www.lemoine-tricote.com

Leutton Postle
leuttonpostle.com

Lucas Nascimento
www.lucasnascimento.com

Missoni
www.missoni.com

Monsieur Lacenaire
www.monsieurlacenaire.com

Nanna van Blaaderen
www.nannavanblaaderen.com

Nikki Gabriel
nikkigabriel.com

Ohne Titel
www.ohnetitel.com

Paolo Errico
www.paoloerrico.com

Pringle of Scotland
www.pringlescotland.com

Sandra Backlund
www.sandrabacklund.com

Sibling
www.siblinglondon.com

Sita Murt
www.sitamurt.com

Somarta
www.somarta.jp

Sonia Rykiel
www.soniarykiel.com

Stine Ladefoged
www.stineladefoged.com

Sumyu Li
www.facebook.com/KnitbySUMYULI

TSE
www.tsecashmere.com

Walter Van Beirendonck
www.waltervanbeirendonck.com

Xavier Brisoux
www.xavierxbrisoux.com

Yang Du
www.yangdu-duyang.com/home.swf

Picture credits

Le Moine Tricote
124–29 © LeMoineTricoteStudio

Leutton Postle
133 Evelyn Kutschera

Lucas Nascimento
136–37, 140, 141 NOW Fashion
138 Pedro Ferraro

Missoni
142 Alasdair McLellan
143–46 MISSONI Archive
147 Juergen Teller

Monsieur Lacenaire
148–53 Benoist Husson,
Vincent Corbillé, Molly Lowe

Nanna van Blaaderen
154–59 Nanna van Blaaderen

Nikki Gabriel
161 Graphic Designer:
Anthony Chiappin
164t Chris Kapa
164b Skeet Booth

Ohne Titel
166–69, 170r, 171t Darren Hall
170l JP Yim

Paolo Errico
172–73 Photographer:
Franceso Brigida, Model: Melinda
174, 176–77 Photographer:
Adriano Russo, Model: Melinda

Pringle of Scotland
181 Worn by Tilda Swinton
for *The Gentlewoman*

Sandra Backlund
184 Calle Stoltz
185, 189t Ola Bergengren
186–87 Peter Gehrke, Care Of
Shotview Photographers,
www.shotview.com
188, 189b Thomas Klementsson

Sibling
190, 195t Thomas Giddings
191 Rob Meyers
193–94 Christopher Dadey

Sita Murt
196–201 Sita Murt

Somarta
202–3,206 Photographer: Sinya
Keita (Roll Up Studio), Art Direction:
Soma Design
204–5 Photographer: Mitsuaki
Koshizuka, Art Direction: Soma Design
207t Art Direction and Movie Design:
Soma Design
207b Photographer: Mitsuaki
Koshizuka, Art Direction and CG:
Soma Design

Sonia Rykiel
208, 210, 212 Frédérique Dumoulin
211 Stéphane Feugère
213 Katja Ralwes

Stine Ladefoged
214–15 Photographer: Niklas
Højlund, Model: Sissel, Styling:
Maria Angelova
217 Photographer: Niklas Højlund,
Models: Emma S & Simone,
Styling: Maria Angelova, Makeup:
Kit Lytjohan.

218, 219b Photographer:
Camilla Reyman, Model: Maria R,
Makeup: Kit Lytjohan

Sumyu Li
220, 225t Fernando Lessa

TSE
226, 228, 230 Ben Weller
227 Anna Thiessen

Walter van Beirendonck
232, 234–35, 237 Dan Lecca
236 Walter van Beirendonck

Xavier Brisoux
238–39, 240, 241b, 242t, 243
Mathieu Drouet
241t Olivier Matton
242b Sketch by Xavier Brisoux
for the Woolmark Prize Collection
'Reminaissance', July 2008.

Yang Du
244–45 Bella Howard
246 Patrick Lindblom
248, 249b Geoff Pugh

Acknowledgements

It has been a joy to research the 40 amazingly talented designers in this book, learning more about established designers and discovering exciting new talent. A huge thank you to these designers for giving up their precious time to be interviewed and for providing me with the inspirational images. Thanks also to the press departments and PR companies that have worked with me to gather information on these designers.

I want to thank all those at Laurence King who have been working on this book, especially Helen Rochester and Melissa Danny. A huge thanks also to Jodi Simpson for your patience and encouragement; it has been a real pleasure to work with you. You really know how to get the best out of your authors.

Thanks to picture researcher Sarah Hopper for all her help in securing all the wonderful images in this book. Thanks also to Venetia Thorneycroft of Praline, who has done such a great job on the design layout.

I have learnt so much about knitwear from my colleagues and friends Wendy Baker and Ted Houghton over the years – thank you for your wealth of specialist knowledge. Thank you to Hywel Davies for encouraging me to write this book, and also to Sid Bryan for his help at the early stages.

A special thanks to my family, in particular my wonderful parents and husband who have looked after Wilf so I could work on this book. I couldn't have done this without your amazing support. To Baz and Wilf, I love you both very much.

Jenny Udale